Falling in Love at the End of the World

FALLING IN LOVE AT THE END OF THE WORLD

STORIES BY
RICK CHRISTMAN

For Lisa:
Thanks for
the
support + good
wishes.
Rick Christman
4/6/94

Minnesota Voices Project Number 62

NEW RIVERS PRESS 1994

Matthew Kluber, the cover artist for *Falling in Love at the End of the World*, is a painter who lives in Cedar Rapids, Iowa. Currently serving as the visiting artist at the Des Moines Art Center, Kluber is a graduate of the Rhode Island School of Design and the University of Iowa.

The publication of *Falling in Love at the End of the World* has been made possible by generous grants from the Dayton Hudson Foundation on behalf of Dayton's and Target Stores, the Jerome Foundation, the Metropolitan Regional Arts Council (from an appropriation by the Minnesota Legislature), the North Dakota Council on the Arts, the South Dakota Arts Council, and the James R. Thorpe Foundation.

Additional support has been provided by the General Mills Foundation, Land o' Lakes, Inc., Liberty State Bank, the McKnight Foundation, the Star Tribune/Cowles Media Company, the Tennant Company Foundation, and the contributing members of New Rivers Press. New Rivers Press is a member agency of United Arts.

New Rivers Press books are distributed by

The Talman Company
131 Spring Street, Suite 201 E-N
New York NY 10012

Falling in Love at the End of the World has been manufactured in the United States of America for New Rivers Press, 420 N. 5th Street/Suite 910, Minneapolis, MN 55401. First Edition.

ACKNOWLEDGEMENTS

"Fire" and "Volleyball" appeared in *Indiana Review*.

"Asylum,""Six Lucky Men," and "Dogs" appeared in *Wormwood Review*.

"When Only Too Long Is Long Enough" appeared in *River City Review*.

"Christmas Holiday" appeared in *Z Miscellaneous*.

"The Mai-Loan and the Man Who Could Fly" appeared in *Great River Review* and *Stiller's Pond: New Fiction from the Upper Midwest* (New Rivers Press).

An excerpt from "Doing Shakespeare" appeared in the *Loft-McKnight Supplement*, a publication in conjunction with the Loft-McKnight Awards.

Several stories appeared in *The Perimeter of Light: Short Fiction and Other Writing about the Vietnam War* (New Rivers Press).

The author would like to particularly thank Vivian Vie Balfour for her superb editorial advice, Matthew Kluber for his artistic expression, and C. W. Truesdale and Katie Maehr for their encouragement and support.

For Dale

CONTENTS

THE BUS CALLING HIS NAME

CHRISTMAS EVE, fresh out of army basic and advanced artillery training, Don sits with five dollars in his pocket in the Milwaukee Greyhound Bus station waiting for the bus that will take him to California to be shipped overseas. From his chair in the dead center of the station he watches a little black girl on her hands and knees, dirtying her pink party dress in the spit and cigarette butts on the floor. He listens to her mother in the seat next to him screech three times for her to stop. Her mother, a huge woman in a bright red dress and orange lipstick, surrounded by suitcases and stuffed paper bags, is paging through an *Ebony* magazine with a picture of Diana Ross and the Supremes on the cover. But the little girl continues to play, heaping cigarette butts into piles, wiping her hands on her dress, until her mother sighs and becomes distracted, dropping her magazine onto her lap. A skinny old black man with a snow white beard sleeps on the other side of Don, his head tipped forward, his lips moving.

* * *

Fourteen days earlier Don arrives on leave in his northern Wisconsin home just in time to discover his mother has embarked on a new life of her own. While he's been gone she's bleached her hair blonde, begun wearing false eyelashes and multi-colored miniskirts, and taken up with a nightshift worker from the pulp mill, across town from her tiny, two-room trailer on the west end.

So Don spends the fourteen evenings of his leave in dreary northern Wisconsin logging bars, draining tap beer after tap beer, toasting the advent of his new life with high school classmates. His classmates bemoan their young lives and laud his as they drink. They tell him how lucky he is to be out of Hurley, Wisconsin, with no responsibilities, no dead end eight to five mill job, no bitching teenage wife, no squawking brats. They look around the dark, identical bars as they talk—red and blue neon beer signs in the windows and on the fake-wood-paneled walls, long tap handles extending over the bars like clubs, grasped over and over by burly, sullen bartenders not interested in the stories or the complaints of their customers. His classmates motion and wave their hands toward old lined men hunched forever over shots of brandy and glasses of Pabst. See what we'll become, they say sadly, pointing to the old men. Tragedy and doom already show in their young eyes like an alcoholic man's Sunday afternoon. Look at us—those old men—that's us sitting over there on those stools. Don's the luckiest man alive, they say. They tell him over and over in bar after bar. They've never seen such luck.

While he's on leave, Don's mother comes into the trailer during the day and sees him in front of the TV, "As the World Turns" going, beer in one hand, cigarette in the other. She asks him shyly, as if she's already forgotten who he is, if he's finding enough to eat, if his leave is going okay. He says sure and notices that one of her false eyelashes is crooked, off center just a bit. He looks closely at her blonde hair, her red miniskirt, her blue and green striped tank top. She's skinny now, where before she was plump and dark-haired, before, when he was eight, before his dad went on his stolen credit card spree across the West, shot to death in a bar near an Indian reservation in South Dakota. At eight, an only child, he imagines his dad, a big man with a broad face, huge nose, and greasy black hair, sidling up next to some dark red Indian woman with braided black hair in a buckskin dress—a squaw—her brave walking in suddenly out of the night, feathers and warpaint, guns blazing. But since Don's been in the army his memories and fantasies concerning his dad are beginning to fade. He remembers him best now in red and blue checkered flannel shirts with a nose so huge he wiped both sides of his face, his eyes, even his ears, after blowing. And sometimes Don remembers sitting on his dad's lap and pinching his dad's great schnoz, then tickling and hugging him until his mother joined in, a pile of hugs and kisses in the middle of the living room floor. But suddenly his father is gone, gone like a puff ball—puff, he is gone. And Don's mother goes to work at the mill and becomes a drudge to raise him. Don knows better than anyone as he grows that she's given up her life for him. They move at once from their white, two-story frame house a mile from town to the shabby trailer court on the west end. As time passes and he finally enters high school, the trailer is no longer big enough for both of them, and he spends his time on the streets, drinking beer underage, fraternizing with whores and pimps and loggers on Silver Street, racing around half the night in wild, careening cars. The later he comes home, the better she seems to like it. She falls asleep every night on the couch—his foldout bed. And when he arrives home, half the morning already gone, she asks nothing of him, but silently heads toward her bedroom, her blue terry cloth robe clutched about her, as if she's in a living trance, as if she's saying to herself over and over, once he's old enough, once he leaves, my life will begin again. He waits impatiently until high school is over and he can get out of town . . . he looks at his mother now, standing only five feet from him, and thinks she's not too bad at that, crooked eyelash and all. This guy from the pulp mill, this nightshift worker, is lucky.

* * *

The little girl plays on. She has built a huge pile, her dress filthy. Her mother has given up completely: she's back to paging through her magazine, looking for Diana Ross. Don is growing fond of the little girl and wishes to get down on his hands and knees and help her with her pile—that pile suddenly seems as important as anything in life. He wants to dirty his pressed green uniform, remove his knotted tie, but he knows he's not wanted in such games any longer. The old man on the other side of him continues sleeping. Don looks at the man's dirty gray suit, wondering vaguely if he's a bum. Even bums should have a place to go on Christmas Eve, he thinks. The man's mouth is working faster in his sleep, on the verge now, it appears, of indiscriminate curses.

Don gets up, grabs his greatcoat, and heads outside onto Michigan Street. He walks a short distance, then leans against the front wall of a building and looks up at the downtown buildings. Even at two in the morning a speaker from somewhere plays Christmas music—"White Christmas," "Good King Wenceslaus," "God Rest Ye Merry Gentlemen," all his favorites.

* * *

His mother is not there to see him off the day he leaves. She leaves him a note on the trailer counter top with a five dollar bill attached to it. She's down the road in Ironwood, she says, with Brad, her nightshift lover, looking for excitement, looking for what she always thought her life was supposed to be like.

I don't want to be hard, the note says, but I don't want you around screwing things up for me now. My luck is finally changing. Besides, she says, you got your own life now. You're old enough to do your own business. Here's five dollars. I wish it was more, but I can't afford more right now. Buy something for the bus. I hope everything goes good for you, I really do. Nothing ever went right for me since your father left, until right now, and I'm almost forty years old. I hope you have better luck than I did.

Don looks at the flyspecked trailer walls and the pile of dishes and greasy pots next to the sink. He stands heavily, as if moored to the floor, while the piles seem to rise, until he can barely see out of the tiny window over the sink. Mill smoke rolls thick, black, and heavy, like artillery tubes, over the dreary town. Finally he stuffs the five dollars into his pocket and heads out of the trailer toward the highway, his green duffel bag banging the door behind him.

* * *

The speaker cracks and the record changes. The needle scratches into "It Came upon a Midnight Clear." Don puts his hands into his greatcoat pockets and watches a dark blue Volkswagen Bug round one corner, head down Michigan Street, round another corner, and disappear. The wind blows down his neck until he shivers and puts his collar up around his ears.

He knows that's the last time he'll ever see Hurley, and he knows it's the last time he'll ever see his mother too. He tries to remember her clearly, maybe for the last time, like she used to be, before her blonde hair, false eyelashes, and miniskirts, before his dad left and ruined all their lives together forever. But he only sees her blonde, faded and skinny in a smoky bar, her skirt half way up her thighs, a glass of beer in her hand, laughing and whirling about, dancing with any man who'll ask her, the time of her life.

Two cars begin drag racing down Michigan Street, shifting, gears grinding, their mufflerless engines drowning out the Christmas music. They're both hopped up Chevrolets, one a green '57 and the other a red '59. Both are customized, chromeless and tilted forward, their backends high into the air, as if they'll dive into the cement at any moment. Don stifles a cheer when the red finally pulls its bumper into the lead, just as they roar out of sight.

Once the noise dies and the music returns, Don notices that a few of the buildings have lights still burning in their upper floors. He wonders absently who's in them, what kind of happy lives they live, what it would be like to be them or just to know them.

He feels a twinge now, a tugging at his arm. He wants to return to the little girl, get down on his knees, play her game. Would she let him? he wonders, would she let him play her game? He wonders, too, where the little girl and her mother are headed, who the old man is cursing, and whether they will all find comfort before this Christmas Eve is over. And finally he wonders if there are others like him, out in the night on an unfamiliar city street with the music of Christmas, with such strange thoughts, such strange feelings, on a night as lonely as this one.

The wind dies, it begins snowing lightly, and from somewhere can be heard the tinkling of bells. He turns his collar back down and stands straight, the snow falling like crystal droplets, like blessings on his head and shoulders.

It's all right to be alone, he decides suddenly, stomping his feet hard one after the other for emphasis, completely alone and on the verge of something. And that's where he is now, after all, on the verge of a new life. In fact, it's the only way to be, no matter what the new life brings.

He scans the tall buildings before him again, the lights from their tiny windows so high in the sky, glowing brightly through the falling snow. He feels himself pull up, strong and invincible. Yes, it's all right to be alone. And he's in good shape, too, he's in fine shape, the best shape ever. He can take care of himself, he knows that. And he has no one to worry about, no one at all.

Don feels power as he has never felt it. He looks at the station and sees through its rough walls. He can scratch his hand down, gouging out cement. He can pull the bricks out one after another if he chooses. He is not afraid of anyone.

The snow continues to fall; the music stops; the city falls silent. He's not sure why he feels as he does, so powerful, so content, but he knows that he will spend the rest of his life trying to feel just this way again. And he knows too that that will all come later and that there is a great deal more to come. And that none of what is to come concerns his mother or his dead father or Hurley, Wisconsin. It concerns exotic lands and big cities, cities bigger than Milwaukee even. There is Chicago and Philadelphia and New York, he knows, yes, and Hong Kong and Bangkok and some with names like no others, names already on the edge of his mind, with no connection, like names out of dreams, names that will become as familiar as his own—Vientiane, Phnom Penh, Luang Prabang, Kom Pong Som, Ia-Drang, Dak To, Da Nang, Hue, and Khe Sanh. But that, he knows, comes later. Now he stands alone, his arms tightly against his sides, his feet close together, his shoulders back—a young soldier on an American city street on Christmas Eve—listening for the only sound in the night, listening for the bus calling his name.

LURP HUMOR

ON THE WEST edge of Bien-Hoa Airbase, next to perimeter Sector A, there was a small LURP detachment of approximately sixty men. They lived out on the end of the base, in fifteen drab, scrubby tents with one Quonset hut latrine, a small unused field separating them from the rest of the base and their nearest comrades. The LURPs crept out over the perimeter every night after dark in pairs, or even alone if the mood struck them, armed with knives, grenades, and shotguns, looking for contact. They liked close combat if possible, the actual feel of flesh against flesh. But if things got too tight, if they ran into more than a squad, they dug in and called air and artillery onto their own positions and lived to tell about it, over and over again.

* * *

The company closest to the LURPs, a field away, next to Sector B, was the 175th Communications Company. The men of the 175th lived and worked in silver air-conditioned trailers with hotplates, refrigerators, stereos, and real beds inside. They had headsets screwed into their heads twenty-four hours a day, strapped around their ears, like giant bugs, twelve hours on, twelve hours off—twelve hours intercepting VC communications, twelve hours of the Rolling Stones, the Animals, and the Jefferson Airplane. Their sandbagged bunkers were dug into the ground beneath their trailers, so when the rockets and mortars began, all they had to do was open the trap door and head down.

But every Monday from eight P.M. until eight Tuesday morning, the men of the 175th Communications Company pulled perimeter guard. They'd be forced out into far bunkers against their wills, armed with M-16s, M-60s, and grenades to guard their sector of the great air base from frequent small arms attacks. Every Monday at eight they'd turn off their radios, remove their headsets, and wait to be moved down the steps of their trailers into formation and out to the perimeter. And every Sunday night, after the shift was over at eight, they'd drink and try to joke about the next night's guard, screaming nervously beyond their headsets and the music, beer foam on their weak moustaches. The attacks on the base had always amazingly come on sectors other than theirs. And they'd look at each other, shake their heads, gulp another beer. We're noncombatants, they'd yell from one to the other, and finish another beer. They'd been trained in basic with old M-14s. They'd never even shot M-16s. They had no idea how.

* * *

But after the first year of the long war, once the LURPs discovered who guarded Sector B every Monday night and Tuesday morning, they devised a favorite game, one they came to love more than anything other than war. They knew that the men of the 175th trembled on guard, any whisper, any hint of noise terrifying them into grabbing the M-16s they couldn't shoot.

So every Tuesday morning around three A.M., if things were slow in the jungle and along the river, they'd sneak back over the perimeter, creep into the back door of each bunker on Sector B, and slip their knives across the exposed throats of the communications company men, laughing—ghoulish white teeth in the awful night. Eventually they'd turn the men loose, but not before flashing cigarette lighters, forcing them to look at fresh ears on their necklaces, the blood on their shirts, a real scrotum sack, or a toe, or a bloody pair of eyes. Then the LURPs would laugh again and head out of the bunkers. Tits on a boar, they'd exclaim. Tits on a boar, you men.

* * *

Finally, of course, after months and years of the war, the men of the 175th Communications Company got used to things as they had come to be; they got used to perimeter guard, to the LURPs sneaking up and threatening to slit their throats nearly every Tuesday morning; they got used to the LURPs' laughter and derision, their souvenir ears and eyes and scrotum sacks. Until, eventually, in this long gone and far away world, the men of the 175th began to wait in anticipation, like they awaited the end of the war or the end of the world, backs to their bunker doorways, white throats vulnerably exposed in the white moonlight, waiting, waiting for the LURPs, their deliverers, for the steel, the slip of the knife.

EMERGENCE

FROM HIS BALCONY seat at the Peking Gardens on Charing Cross, Klein sees eels entwined, twisting, turning, bumping against the lid of the glass tank on the third floor landing. He hears Chinese customers on the floor below, scraping chopsticks and banging plates. An English couple argues at another balcony table: He should have known she wanted to go, she should have known he didn't. The man smiles down on the woman's beautiful blonde head, wondering how much longer he will be able to tolerate such a fool.

* * *

Marion married Klein, a Vietnam-obsessed heavy drinker, ten years ago for no good reason that Klein knows, and ever since has been financing his sporadic university attendance and restless searches to find someone to forgive him. He picks up and leaves whenever one of his urges to search possesses him, runs off frantically to the oddest places, places chosen for no apparent reason, sometimes taking her with him, when she can get time off from her job as an accountant for a law firm, and sometimes taking only her money, the urges so strong that he is yanked along without choice, like a kite in a strong wind, his feet barely touching the ground.

Klein studied Vietnamese at the army's famous language

school at the Presidio of Monterey, then spent three years as an interrogator with the First Infantry Division at Dian. He interrogated prisoners from 6:30 in the morning on, for as long as they brought them in, some blindfolded, some with eyes searching the ground, others with heads twisted into the air, arms lashed behind them, elbows pointed at their backs. He interrogated them all the same, after they were brought to his little shack in the middle of the dusty, barbed-wire, P.O.W. compound.

* * *

The English couple leaves and is replaced at once by one so similar that, if Klein hadn't seen the other one leave in a taxi, he'd think they had left and come back again. He finishes his half pint of lager and quickly orders another. Lunch is concluding, the banging and scraping has decreased drastically below. Klein gulps his new beer: They'll want him to drink fast now, he knows. He looks around at the slim, simply dressed Chinese waiters and wonders if they can help him, as he watches one leap the stairs two at a time, remove the glass lid, grasp an eel in a wire snare, and bring it squirming and snapping out of the water.

* * *

The prisoners didn't talk at first, of course, whether terrified or defiant, and his aides, Sergeant Tuan and Corporal Tam, did the softening up. He didn't want to know their methods, and Sergeant Tuan and Corporal Tam were extremely ingratiating to their American counterpart. They did anything to accommodate him, anything at all. His aides looked exactly alike to him, and he wouldn't have been able to tell them from the prisoners—their faces yellow and foreign and slanted, their features soft and delicate, like women—if it hadn't been for their immaculately pressed uniforms, their black Ranger berets cocked just so. He always had to glance at their rank stripes to tell which was Sergeant Tuan and which was Corporal Tam.

Once his men set to work on the first group of prisoners, he left the shack and went to his silver, air-conditioned trailer, turned his stereo system on three quarter volume, and lay on his bed with a cold beer. Later, Sergeant Tuan or Corporal Tam knocked and entered smiling, but with a hint of regret that it was finished so soon, and informed him that it was time: The prisoners were ready to talk.

* * *

Banging back on the subway to meet Marion, Klein thinks he sees her boss leering arrogantly down the car, clutching a woman's purple-stockinged thigh. Two green-haired lovers nestle across from him, wrapped together in rope, encased in mesh webbing. Staring ahead out of the train window at the sliding dark, he begins seeing unused subway lines and abandoned subway stops, black metal and gray stone structures twisted in agony, like an obsolete life buried beneath his own.

* * *

When he re-entered the shack, he was amazed how the prisoners begged him to listen, to hear what they had to say. He barely got inside the door of the shack before the first prisoner began babbling, often grabbing onto his sleeve for dear life. Then he allowed their faces melt into talking mouths until he was finished with them: A division here, a division there, a communications net on a hill. All that mattered was that they talked, that he had something to pass on; whether it was true or not was no concern of his.

Once he finished, he returned again to his silver trailer, lay on his bed, and let the air conditioning blow over him, the music pounding from his stereo, drinking beer after beer from the refrigerator at his right hand, until he fell asleep. Then, on his way back to the shack in the morning, he saw them, yesterday's work, squatting together on the hard ground in the barbed-wire compound, awaiting transportation to the permanent prison camp, vacant and brown, like discarded cardboard boxes empty forever, blown by the wind into the gathering dust. And as the days passed one upon another, so simple and so mesmerizing, he sank deeply into his routine and felt he could go on with it for the rest of his life, until he forgot everything else, until it became all he ever knew.

* * *

As he rides the steep escalator out of the depths of the Underground, he feels in danger of falling and nearly clutches the woman in front of him. She turns back to him, feeling his breath on her neck. Then, grasping her shopping bags more tightly, she begins rising above him to the colors of Oxford Street, step after step to the top.

* * *

Once the war ended and Klein left Vietnam for good, the strangest thing happened. Once he left, his Vietnamese left him abruptly, too. And once it left him, it left him utterly. He could rack his brain all he wanted, nothing would come; he couldn't remember a single word. He couldn't even speak a few syllables to people who yapped at him through the years:

"Come on, say something in Gook. Come on, speak, speak, come on."

And when he encountered Vietnamese living in America, he discovered that he couldn't bear to look at them, much less recall a word or two. His throat would get dry and he would slink into a corner, eyes downcast, a creepy feeling coursing up his spine. Until finally, he took his loss as a sign of his sin and corruption and became obsessed, searching the country, thinking that if he somehow found one Vietnamese at the right time, in the right place, he would remember everything and be forgiven.

* * *

He enters a clothing store to capture a brief respite from the saturation of life on Oxford Street. A clerk approaches at once and Klein tries on piles of sweaters of red, blue, and green. But within seconds the door opens and people stream in; clerks carom about the store from one to another. Finally, Klein flees, his new green sweater rolled and wrapped in brown paper, clutched like a shotgun under his arm.

* * *

And then Marion had married him and he'd thought, Oh, what the hell, he could use her money. And even their honeymoon had been one of his searches. Maybe things would be different in Europe, he thought, yes, maybe Europe would be just the thing. He knew there were many Vietnamese living in Paris. Maybe there his tongue would loosen, maybe giving vent again to the restlessness and searching that plagued him would finally alleviate his tongue-tied condition, maybe the Vietnamese there would make him remember.

Their first night in Paris it rained, but they hustled through street after unfamiliar street, searching frantically for that one perfect restaurant. Marion stared out from under her rain-drenched hood, beseeching him to find a restaurant, any restaurant, but he was determined.

Finally he found what he wanted on a gray, Right Bank street —The Imperial Restaurant Vietnamein. They entered cautiously, hung their raincoats and found seats. But he couldn't read the French menu and there was nothing in Vietnamese. It came to him then—too late—how stupid it had been of him to think that there would be a Vietnamese menu in Paris.

The young Vietnamese owner took one look at them and asked him in pidgin English what they wanted. He strutted and postured before their table. Klein was humiliated and, of course, couldn't respond with a single word of Vietnamese. He bumbled ahead in English, forgetting the main course. While they ate, the owner smoked cigarettes with limp-wristed sophistication, fawning outrageously over a table of French diners nearby. And the food was Chinese.

* * *

Klein seats himself at the Museum Tavern after securing their pints of ale and notices that Marion has curled her hair about her face, the way he once told her he likes it. As he takes his first drink, he discovers that he has been right.

* * *

And now, ten years after she married Klein, Marion has taken a lover, her complacent, puce-colored, lawyer boss. Klein knows this because for the past year he has skipped classes nearly every day and followed her to work, watching them attentively through their office window. He has gotten into his car and followed them off to restaurants and delicatessens for lunch. From a hidden table he has watched them nuzzle each other and squeeze hands, whispering and making plans. He has watched her kiss the cheeks of his round bowling-ball head—squeezed off from his string ties— exuding success, certainty and confidence, perfection in his lawyer world. He has seen his dark red hands move, directing movements of waiters, waitresses, and cooks. He has felt her silence and pale-ghost movements throughout their house, imagining her thoughts of love, music, and romance.

*　*　*

Klein watches one of the bartenders come out from behind the bar and walk over to the white lunch case in the corner. The woman who runs the counter is placing cellophane over dishes of cold salads and cold meats, preparing to leave shortly. She wears a white dress, similar to a nurse's uniform, filling it out to the absolute fullest with her hips and breasts. The bartender, a man half her size, stands next to her on tiptoes, whispering out of the side of his mouth until she throws her head back and roars. She places a matronly hand on his shoulder, patting him in time as they continue laughing and whispering.

Klein looks up at Marion and sees her mouth moving. People disappear to him once he turns his head—even Marion. When he's in another room, he forgets what she looks like. When she calls to him, it's like a strange voice out of the night. But for no reason that he knows, her eyes stand out indelibly, shockingly, to him now and he wonders at how green they are.

She has given him up, her boss, her lover; it was just a momentary fling. It was nothing. It won't happen again.

Klein drinks and watches the other bartender fuss with his bottles, then reach quickly for the bar towel and wipe a smudge off of the back mirror. He is tall and broad with the aloof, impenetrable appearance of many British bartenders, his sideburns completely covering the sides of his face, like pictures Klein once admired—drunk—of John L. Sullivan, on the walls of an Irish bar in Boston. The bartender moves like a boxer, too, his arms long and agile on the pressure taps, light on his feet as he moves behind the oak.

She's been offered another job, a better one, for another lawyer, and she's going to take it. Then she won't even be near him anymore.

Klein finishes his beer and gets another. He reseats himself and watches a black and white couple who've taken seats next to them, sipping white wine delicately, as if their lips might fasten permanently to their glasses. Klein doesn't believe what is happening, what he's been hearing, but he'll take what he can get. As

Marion continues talking, he notices she is wearing her large, horn-rimmed glasses and realizes that he has always liked her better in them than in her contact lenses. He sees, too, that the spaces between her small teeth make her look innocent, though as he listens to her continue, she rapidly becomes eloquent, eloquent and insightful beyond either of their natures.

She feels she is dirty and contemptible, filthy with immorality, like she has sinned and cannot be pardoned. She knows it's not too much to say that she has somehow shaken the fabric of the world in what she has done, and that nothing can be the same ever again. She suggested this trip to London, hoping that travel would make everything all right, but she knows now that is impossible. But she would go anywhere or do anything to make it right again if she could, to have it to do all over again. Can he ever forgive her, she asks.

She is so shaken now by her own eloquence and insight that she seems possessed, her beautiful green eyes magnified even larger by her glasses, her hands flat, gripping the table, as she leans forward, until their beer glasses begin sliding toward her and tears begin to smear the make-up beneath her eyes, lightening the color of her cheeks.

Klein wants badly to reach over and grasp Marion's hair in his hands, crushing her soft cheeks to him over the table, smashing glass, rattling and shaking and remolding the essence of their lives across time. But he knows that it is too late for that now.

A small dog scoots out from around the bar and heads for Klein and Marion. He barks and yaps, standing on his hind legs, begging before them. Klein looks from the dog to Marion. She is sitting back in her chair, grinning sheepishly, hand outstretched. Klein smiles, too, and picks the dog up onto his lap, caressing it. Marion reaches over and pats the dog gingerly on the nose.

Out on the street the rush-hour traffic is in full force—double-decker buses and taxicabs battle for the streets like the end of the world is at hand. But Klein and Marion leave the Museum Tavern and begin walking down Great Russell Street as if they are strolling a country lane. As they walk, they seem pushed above the diesel fuel, above the rush-hour noise and sights around them, somehow insulated from the colors and sounds of real life. The Museum itself looms silently across the street, as if it sits on a hill, massive, possessing the earth above them. His ears begin ringing in this black and white world and he wonders if she, too, is affected, when suddenly, she reaches out and squeezes his arm with the truth. Yelling *come on* she runs toward a doubledecker bus as his heart leaps and he runs as fast as he can to catch her.

THE WHORE, THE LINGUIST, AND THE GREEN BERET

THE WHORE WORKED the Elysee Bar on a sidestreet off Nguyen-Hue, her exceptional beauty melting all the soldiers' hearts into lust, even those grunts who hated all Vietnamese because they spent so much time killing them. When they would see the whore, they would slide into the chair next to her like candlewax. And the whore would hold their hands until they giggled like schoolboys on a picnic.

The linguist was only nineteen when he met the whore his first payday, the day after he had been in country for two weeks. It was his first night out in Saigon, and he just walked in off the street. He wanted a beer and he wanted to practice his newly-acquired language skills.

When the linguist saw the whore, he grabbed onto the bar, his legs shaking. Eventually he was able to sit down, take all the money out of his wallet, and lay it on the table in front of the whore, over three hundred and fifty dollars.

She should take what she needed, the linguist told her in his best Vietnamese. He wanted her and she could take it all, if that's what it took.

The whore looked down at the money spread out in a lovely profusion of colors—tan MPCs, green, red, and blue piasters. She looked at the linguist, his eyes filled with lust and youth. She knew a virgin when she saw one and a virgin was good luck. All right, come along, then, she said.

The whore led the linguist down a dark, creepy alley and up darker, creepier stairs. They stopped before a door off a dreary hallway that smelled of *nuoc-mam* and masturbation. The whore knocked and opened the door. She smiled at the linguist. Her family, she said.

She chased the people out of the room and into the hallway: a limping grandma and grandpa, a meek mother and father, babies in the arms of small children. They stumbled out, sleep in their eyes, and stretched out on the hallway floor, twelve of them.

After the linguist and the whore had finished, the whore got out of bed and called them all back in. They curled up everywhere. One lay on a table against the wall. The father began to snore and a child rolled fitfully about on the floor. A baby moaned and gurgled softly. The linguist lay still, watching and listening. A breeze blew in through an open window and tickled his chest hairs.

In the middle of the night, a black Green Beret entered the room and pointed a .45 pistol to the linguist's head. She was his girl, the Green Beret said. He leaned over the bed, his head like a black balloon. The room filled with bourbon breath. She was pregnant and she was his girl. She had already had one of his kids. The Green Beret snapped a flashlight into the linguist's eyes and then shined it on the whore next to him. Oh my God, the Beret said, he was sorry. It was a big mistake.

An hour after the Green Beret left, the bedbugs attacked. They bit and bit until the blood ran down the linguist's arms and legs in small streams. He squirmed and scratched, but the bugs continued to bite.

When dawn streaked against the yellow wall, the linguist smelled what he knew must be gonorrhea. He swung quickly out of bed, dropping his feet heavily onto the floor. His feet grazed a child's head, actually caressing its peach fuzz. The whore had not moved all night, and he watched as the morning breeze blew the Saigon streets in through the open window. Her silky hair lifted and ruffled around her beautiful face as if she were flying.

Later, when the linguist told his coworkers about his first night out, they laughed lasciviously and poked him good-humoredly in the ribs and testicles. They called him a sly young lecher, a true Saigon Warrior. He grinned with embarrassment and happiness. By late afternoon he could hardly wait until shift change.

THE MAI-LOAN AND THE
MAN WHO COULD FLY

EARLIER THAT NIGHT, the same night Sing met the man who could fly, one of the hotel waiters told about his wife who got killed by a gunship at the Cholon Racetrack the week before. It seemed she was taking a shortcut on the way to the market when the gunner opened up. Sing imagined a leer on the gunner's face, like arousal, straddling his machine gun and pumping lead from between his legs like the seed of heavenly death. The fifty caliber cut her in half, and the waiter had to go to the Body Reclamation Center to identify her and claim her remains and only one half of her was there. The other half somehow got away from them en route and hadn't been found yet.

The whores playing cards at the corner table erupted into a violent argument, and Sing turned and watched them closely and deliberately. One slammed her cards onto the table and stood with hands on hips, ranting furiously at the others. It wasn't Kim but he kept watching anyway, as her long black hair bounced against her cheeks, her head snapping from one to another. The others were cheats, she said, in league against her. They talked behind her back. They took customers from her. They hated her, she said. But soon she was cajoled into continuing the game that went on and on as always, from the time the bar opened in the morning until it closed at night.

The waiters always talked about dead wives or dead sons or

20

daughters, and Sing enjoyed listening to their stories, their voices, as he watched the flares float and the red tracers spit across the river. He was soothed by the familiar drone of their heartache, as he was soothed by the distant color of the war across the river. The waiter was crying now, of course, and Sing noticed for the first time how the tears on the waiter's cheeks were like delicate chips of the finest, handblown glass. He considered this, considered sitting forward and looking more closely, maybe even reaching out to touch, to see if they were genuine. But he knew without even beginning that he wasn't capable.

The eighth floor bar had been a classy place once; the round bar had twinkled with polished glass and suspended bottles; snappy, insistent, French-speaking waiters had rushed food and drinks, the room spinning and aswirl about the rich, the spies, and the journalists, at balcony tables among potted trees. But by the time Sing met the man who could fly, the war had dulled the polish and chipped the balcony pots, and the waiters lounged and ate openly before the customers. By that time it had become another half-baked restaurant and bar, another hangout for whores and pimps and the trafficking of drugs, though some of the waiters amused one another by still speaking French among themselves, as if to act out just how far life had come.

The night Sing met the man who could fly, it was three years since he had arrived at the Mai-Loan, three years since he had been an interpreter and interrogator with the First Marines. He came down to Saigon on a three-day R&R; his unit, what was left of the eighteen who had gone out—the medic, the radio operator, and himself, was awarded the rest along with the Bronze Star for salvaging themselves from an ambush that brought them so much more than they expected. The fifteen others dropped one after another in seconds, but the three of them were invincible. As the men they knew best on earth dropped dead, the three of them felt a power move within. They walked right out into the bush and scattered the others. They were actually close enough to see the eyes of the enemy, bulging in the face of such audacity and sacred power.

For the three days on R&R they couldn't look at each other, and they couldn't talk of anything else. They couldn't whore, they couldn't drink anything but Coke. The whores and the pimps kept their distance, and didn't even attempt to break the sacred ring the three men had established. Even the street kids and the beggars were driven away by their hollow, possessed looks, edging by to allow them plenty of room, crossing the street way up ahead when they saw the three of them coming.

They couldn't talk about anything but the dumb, dead motherfuckers, as they walked down the street, as they sat in bars, the expressions on the faces of the dead, their arms akimbo or stretched above their heads just so, their legs twisted, the color of their blood, their eyes round and wide and wet, like sliced cucumbers. And the three of them, the only three noncombatants in the whole Marine Corps probably, the only three who didn't carry rifles had finally picked up rifles for the first time. And there they were. And all the others, those trained, hardened killers, those dumb fuckers were dead. They shook their heads. They couldn't believe it. They talked day and night, in their enlisted men's quarters after curfew, in one of their rooms, on one of their beds. They talked because they couldn't sleep.

Then the night before they were to leave, they left each other at 10:30, giving each a few hours alone before the 7:00 A.M. flight back to Phu-Bai and the two hour mail truck ride back to the unit. Sing walked the streets until 11:00 o'clock curfew, ending up on the eighth floor bar at the Mai-Loan. He took a balcony seat and watched the lights of the war across the river, sipping a *Ba-Muoi-Ba*, the tracers, the flares, the bombs, so far away, so long gone in the night. He sat mesmerized and dreamy, his beer gone, his head resting back against the chair, until the bartender shut off the lights and a waiter tapped his shoulder. Sing bought a room down the hall for the night and didn't leave the eighth floor for three years.

* * *

Sing's father had been a marine, too. He'd been shot in the head in the Pacific and still carried a steel plate that on certain cloudy days, when something in the air was just right, rolled his eyes back in his head, lighting him up inside like a Christmas tree. And every Christmas Eve, once the tree had been purchased from Birch's Greenhouse, propped in Sing's wagon and dragged the eight blocks back to their house through snow-wet northern Wisconsin streets, and before the tree was on the stand and placed in the spot in front of the bay window for decorating, his father stood with arms extended, legs spread-eagled, a green Christmas tree bulb in each hand and a red one in his mouth. And as his only child looked on in delight, he asked out beyond the bulb like a 1920s gangster, "Hell, we don't need a tree, do we, son?"

But his father's patriotism was so extreme and tinged with such terror and violence that it was nearly as if his father wished the bullet had killed him for his country, almost as if he were ashamed it hadn't. He lectured his only child on the corruption of the young and the loss of men with real balls in this crumbling world. A vein stuck out prominently in his forehead once he got started. He pointed at the television for illustration, ranting and raging for hours at the hippies, the pussies, and the sissies. He exhorted Sing constantly to keep his head high, to eat the good food his mother prepared, to keep his eyes open at all times and to never back down from a good fight. But always fight to kill, no matter who it was, no matter what. Grab the nearest rock if he needed to. People were out to get him, he said. Don't trust anyone. Always hold something back for reserve.

From the time Sing was eight, his father moved all the furniture out of the living room every evening and every Saturday afternoon and taught his son hand-to-hand combat on the living room rug. By the time Sing was twelve he could gouge, rip, and choke his classmates at the least provocation. But he discovered as he grew older that he didn't want to rip his classmates' throats out. He worshiped his father as he thundered through the house like Goliath, and he tried his hardest to do anything his father wished him to do. But away from the house Sing found himself reading books, liking his teachers, and even secretly playing jump rope with girls. He grew straddling the world and enlisted in the Marines to please his father, but refused to carry a rifle to please himself. He didn't want to come home from the war as his father had, a hater of the world with buzzers in his head.

* * *

Sing's second night at the Mai-Loan one of the whores left her card game to come and sit next to him at his table. Her name was Kim, she said. She talked for two hours about her dead mother and father and two little brothers. She moved her long, miniskirted legs back and forth from time to time as she talked. She had been working these three long years just to get them all out of there alive, away from the war, away from Vietnam forever. But now she spit on Vietnam forever, she said, because they were dead, killed that very week in their house on Truong-Ming-Ky. She could see how it had been for them, she said, splattered like mice in a barrel as they ran from wall to wall for refuge, scratching the dirt floor for the basement that wasn't there. As she talked, her angular, hollow-eyed face seemed drained, yet still longing for marrow and blood and human life. She finished by telling him that she would hire him as her protection if he wished. She didn't need it, but you never knew. She didn't care about money for herself anymore. Then she returned to her game and never spoke to him again.

So Kim took Sing on as her protection, though in his three years there he had to think about protecting her only once. An American civilian found his way up to the eighth floor bar, got drunk, and began punching Kim in the eyes and mouth with short, professional-boxer-like jabs and chopping right hands. There was no sound at all, other than the slap of skin and bone against skin and bone, and Kim was too amazed to even shout for him. So by the time Sing saw what was going on, the bartender broke the man's head with a chunk of lead pipe he kept behind the bar.

Sing slept late every morning and all afternoon read the Vietnamese newspapers, brought to him each day at noon along with his cigarettes by the twelve-year-old Mai-Loan doorguard, drug dealer, and pimp in a turned up jungle hat with a Benson and Hedges 100 drooping from his chin to his shirt buttons. Then, from two o'clock in the afternoon on, Sing sat at his balcony table drinking Canadian Club chased with *Ba-Muoi-Ba*. Before the bartender shut out the lights at midnight and went home, he left a bottle of whiskey and five bottles of warm beer lined up on Sing's table. After the bar was closed and dark and everyone was gone, Sing's glass clinked as he poured more whiskey and his cigarette hung down along the side of his chair until it burned his fingers and he put it out to light another. He drank and stared out the window until dawn, trying to remember if there ever was a time when there was anything but war across the river.

Kim supplied Sing's room, his newspapers, his food, his liquor, his cigarettes, and his one set of clothes. She could afford him, she was the best whore in the place. No one could compete with her lean dark beauty. They had few customers up on the eighth floor, but the best of those who came, came to Kin, and they paid what she demanded, no matter how outrageous her price of the moment was, pulling handfuls of piasters and black market MPCs from their pockets in green, red, blue, and tan profusion like Christmas. Even her most timid requests brought offers of cameras, refrigerators, radios, and cars.

Kim told the waiters to pay attention to Sing's needs. They knew when he wanted a drink and when he was hungry. He ate what all the help ate, when they ate it. He shaved every third day but kept his blond hair long, like Custer, cutting it only every six months by chopping handfuls off with a razor-sharp, bone-handled kitchen knife. He wore a black pajama shirt and black pajama pants. He hadn't said twenty-five words in three years.

* * *

The waiter left and the man who could fly settled in at the seat across from Sing's table. Sing was mildly disturbed, but the man who could fly began talking at once, as soon as he settled in. He talked on and on, his monologue weaving and bending and wrapping around Sing's head like an insistent, evil snake.

Sing couldn't see the man who could fly very well, though he was only five feet from him; he couldn't seem to make him out. Sing looked back across the river and listened, the flares bursting, the bombs falling, the war continuing.

The man who could fly said the war had seen its better days. It will end soon, he said. There was no doubt about it, now that the American pullout had begun, no doubt at all. Soon, very soon, the Vietcong will have things their way. They will make the country strong, they will make it Vietnamese again. And high time, too, he said, high time. They will ride into Saigon like the heroes they are, like the French Resistance liberating Paris. The revolution will come, finally it will come. Vietnam will cleanse itself of American filth and degradation. The people will hold their heads high again. The whores and pimps and bartenders will be marched into the sea.

The man who could fly waved his hand dramatically over the table between them. Sing could barely make out a smile on his insubstantial face.

He had just come from Nha-Trang and the collaborators were fleeing down Highway One in droves, their oxcarts clipclopping, banging out music to the revolutionary's ears. And the Americans were already gone from Nha-Trang, their huge air base deserted. They were disappearing from bases everywhere, all over Vietnam, as if someone had passed a magic wand over the country, as if someone had finally pulled the plug.

With great effort Sing turned toward the bar. He wished the man who could fly would disappear and let him be once again. He was uncomfortable now. For the first time in three years he was disturbed by a bee on glass, by a bee which refused to go away. But finally, when Sing looked back again, the man who could fly really had disappeared. Sing looked all around the room and out over the river and the street below. He seized his chair arms and wondered suddenly if he, too, might fly out the window.

* * *

For the first time in three years Sing returned to his room before the bar closed. He entered and went directly out onto the small, cement balcony without even bothering to turn on the light. He leaned out against the cement railing and ran his fingers along its roughness. The breeze in his hair made him feel lightheaded. He looked at the sky and the river and the street below. He saw a sampan filled with children and a withered old man. It bobbed and rolled and pitched forward on the end of the anchor rope, as the helpless old man pulled and pulled on the rope with all his skinny might, the children rocking from one end of the boat to the other. Down the street a tiny blue and white taxicab was parked, the driver and his fare—a black marine—both gesturing in the middle of the street, oblivious to the traffic careening about them. On the curb in front of the hotel, an emaciated *xich-lo* driver talking with another marine suddenly threw both hands into the air and laughed all the way to heaven. Sing watched the doorguard below slip money into his shirt pocket with one hand and extend a pack of cigarettes with the other. And in the center of the street, in his tiny kiosk, a White Mouse directed traffic, his white-gloved hands moving in perfect coordination, orchestrating, pointing and directing each in turn.

Sing read of the American withdrawal in the Vietnamese newspapers, but he never believed them. They were fairyland: movie stars, gossip columns, husband advertisements, created sources and government control. He never took them seriously for a moment, especially the warnings of an imminent Saigon surrender. But he saw the enemy come now, moving down the street, a great tangled blade of iron—tanks, jeeps, trucks, Freedom Fighters atop armored personnel carriers, brandishing weapons and crying their maniacal love of Ho—heading down Le-Loi to the end and back again. And back again and again and again.

Sing looked out across the river, grabbed the balcony railing, and gathered himself up on his toes like God. Huge balls of light from parachute flares popped and floated down the sky like eyes, and strings of red tracers wound round and round and up and down. He couldn't help himself. He began thinking of Christmas Even in snow-wet city streets and of Christmas trees of red and green. He released the balcony railing and rocked back on his feet, letting his hands hang at his sides. He shivered and shook like bamboo as he felt the wind rush by his face, already picking up his long hair like fingers.

SIX LUCKY MEN

AT BIEN-HOA, the popularity of the garbage run was legend. Every Thursday, six men would be chosen to ride shotgun atop a heaped deuce-and-a-half to a jungle dumping ground. Their purpose, other than riding shotgun in the event of an enemy attack, was to open the tailgate and push the garbage out with their snow shovels. The six were chosen by roster.

But the real reason for the garbage run's popularity with the men was the garbage run game. Long ago, no one knew exactly when, the game had been invented by some of the men who had preceded them. The game was financed by the company's enlisted men's club. For every beer or shot of whiskey sold, ten cents in MPCs was thrown into a box that became known as the Garbage Run Pool.

Each run was allotted two cases of bar soap and a case of Coke for ammunition. Once the six men chosen were finished with their garbage duties, they would break open the cases, sit up along the sides of the deuce-and-a-half box, and peg Coke cans and soap bars at the scavengers.

Ten cents was awarded for a hit, twenty cents for the genitals, fifty cents for the head, and five dollars for a knock out. There would be the usual arguments over who hit whom where, but they would never argue seriously. They had too much fun to be serious.

And the scavengers were like huge rats to the men, huge rats with yellow teeth and squinty black eyes. They would dig around with their bags dragging behind them, hunched over, like all the old men and women who haunt town dumps everywhere, pelted with rocks and taunted by children.

And since the scavengers welcomed the Coke and soap as potential black market merchandise, they made excellent targets. When the throwing would begin, they would stand exposed, their arms at their sides, their legs wide apart, and their crotches thrust forward. They knew a good thing when they saw one; they knew what the men were after.

And sometimes fights would break out among the scavengers over a bar of soap or a Coke, or over some half-eaten sandwich or half-full can of vegetables. They would hit each other with their fists and claw at each other's eyes. They would bite and scream and wail like banshees.

Once the six men returned to the company, triumphantly riding the sides of the truck, their weapons brandished like the Resistance entering Paris, they would collect their money and spend all afternoon and evening in the club, drinking their winnings.

And it probably would have continued forever, except that one raucous afternoon in '70, the week's lucky six went out drunk without their Coke and soap and played the game for real.

TALKING

EVERY MORNING AFTER the postcard arrived three weeks ago, Lang walked down to the lake at 6:00 A.M. and sat out on the end of the pier until dark. The pier was a ten block walk down Sherman Avenue from his apartment on Gorham Street, and he walked it rapidly, trying not to look up at the huge houses that loomed above him on the old street. Sherman Avenue had formerly been the absolute fashion center of the city, but by that time had degenerated into two rows of crumbling, shabby houses divided into apartments. He could imagine each one exploding as he walked, blown one upon another in his mind, bricks falling, roofs caving in, much like the shabby crumbling of his own life.

The pier was a long one, stretching out a hundred yards into the blue lake. From its end Lang could look around the curve of the lake at the hotels and high-rise campus buildings from a different perspective, until they appeared part of a country so foreign that nothing reminded him of the postcard and the past. He could spend the whole day ignoring them in the blue water.

But once dark came and he returned to his apartment, the postcard was always there on the kitchen counter top, white enough to reflect light, staring back at him and demanding attention, like it had eyes. "We'll be arriving at 9:00 A.M., June 3rd. I'll come by your apartment after supper, about 7:00. I can hardly wait to see you again and talk over old times (and keep warm!). Love, Anne."

* * *

Lang returned fresh from Ia-Drang Valley in September of '67, remembering of the end only the bounce and rush of the plane and the cries and uproarious clapping of his comrades, as they burst out into the cold air and fell on their knees to kiss the concrete runway of the country that had nearly killed them. He never even bothered to return to his northern Wisconsin home, but began school at once. His father had died when he was twelve and his mother when he was in basic training. He signed up for his monthly G.I. Bill allotment and used his separation pay to rent an apartment, pay tuition, and buy books and clothes. He settled in in two days.

On the Monday classes began, as he headed down the street in an old fatigue shirt, someone threw a full box of Kleenex out a passing car window and hit him in the stomach. He doubled over and spilled his books all over the cement. A block further down the street a car backfired and he dove for cover into a nearby hedge. Later, in his first class—political science—an ex-marine stood and began emotionally defending his role as a naive seventeen-year-old in the A-Chau Valley. The class rose in unison, like a dance chorus, and booed and hooted him right out the door.

After classes Lang returned to his apartment and locked and chained the door. He switched on the television, put his feet up on the coffee table and popped a quart of J&B. He drank and watched television and ate bologna sandwiches. By three o'clock when he climbed into bed he was firm in his mind. It was as if he had died and been born again on another planet, he decided, without any experience at all. The war was all he remembered—it had been so all-consuming and he had been only seventeen—the only experience he had. But now, since he allowed himself to remember little of that, since he blocked that out almost totally— his reaction to the backfiring car had just been a well-conditioned reflex—everything was playing for the first time. He lay in the dark and stared at the ceiling. But he had learned something already. No one had to know anything. He would tell no one, and no one would ever know. He imagined the rest of his life a pro-

cession of days and nights just like this afternoon and evening
had been. He was content imagining it so.

After that night Lang stopped wearing old fatigue shirts. He
went to classes and returned to his apartment immediately after-
ward. He bought groceries and liquor at the Gorham Street Cor-
ner Market and returned with his staples at once. He watched
television, drank J&B, and paid his rent by mail. He didn't speak
a word to anyone.

But one Friday afternoon in early April, the first warm day of
spring, as he was heading to his apartment down University
Avenue toward Gorham Street, he stopped in front of the 602
Club bar. He had passed the place twice a day for six months, to
and from school, but today was the first time he stopped. He felt
the sun on his flannel shirt as he stood in the middle of the side-
walk. The air smelled exciting. It was a Friday afternoon after
school in the spring time, a day nothing could go wrong. He
looked up at the green wooden sign with "602" carved unevenly
into it. He walked to the entrance and looked in through the
screened door. He could smell beer, cigarette smoke, and old
wood. He shifted his books to the other arm.

Lang sat on a stool next to the front window, ordered a
schooner of beer, and lit a Pall Mall. He turned in his stool and
looked around the dark, pale-green bar. He recognized his
physics professor—a stocky, bearded man all in black, only his
face and hands breaking the black smudge—talking intently at
the end of the bar with a young man with a blond ponytail and a
beautiful face. There were rows of green booths along each wall
of the back room and long, formica-topped tables jammed into
the space between. Two gray-haired men played cribbage at one
of the tables, a bearded student with them, his bookbag hanging
off his chairback. They whooped and insulted each other good-
naturedly as the men moved the pegs up and down the board.

Lang turned and looked at himself in the mirror behind the bar.
He tipped his head and felt behind his collar. His light brown hair
was beginning to grow long, and he had grown a beard, which to
his surprise had come out black. He turned away. He didn't even
have to look in the mirror to shave anymore.

He ordered another beer and a package of Pall Malls and
watched the bartender move from the tap, to the old, wooden cig-
arette dispenser, back to the spot at the bar in front of him. Lang

lay all his money out on the bar and let the bartender take what was necessary. Lang was just another student. He could be anyone.

An hour later a man and a woman entered with guitar cases and stood along the bar next to Lang's stool. They ordered drinks and continued to stand, their cases next to their feet. They sipped their drinks and talked quietly.

Later, the woman asked Lang if they could store their cases for a time, out of the way, next to the wall by the other side of his stool. He nodded his head and she smiled at him. Thank you, she said.

Later still, she turned to Lang again, smiling, a tiny mouth with perfect white teeth. Her hair was long and straight and her forehead high. Her eyes squinted and made lines when she smiled, like the quick meow of a cat. Did he come here often? No? They never came here. The place always looked creepy to them. It was their first time. They were musicians, obviously. She laughed. She and Skip, here, her husband. They were on their way to a gig at eight-thirty, and they stopped here on the way. The Brat and Brau on Regent, did he know it? No? Right on Regent, across from University Apartments.

The first time Lang opened his mouth his voice cracked, but in no time at all it was running smoothly again. Soon they were talking and drinking comfortably, like old friends. She wanted to know this, she wanted to know that. They lived in an apartment on the eastside, off Atwood. Did he know where Atwood was? No, he was new in town and didn't get around much. She went to school, music, of course, and Skip, here, her husband, worked at University Hospitals as a janitor. They needed the money, she shrugged. But they would make it soon, she added quickly, rising to her tiptoes. They were on the verge now for sure.

She moved even closer to Lang as they talked. She looked at him warmly, even seductively, it seemed. She squeezed his arm often and laughed. He was almost sure at one point that he felt her warm thigh caress the side of his leg, and even though he knew it couldn't be, he looked at her perfect teeth, and nearly forgot that her husband, Skip, was there.

Later, at 8:00, she invited Lang to attend their performance at the Brat and Brau after 9:00, then she and her husband left, guitar cases banging the door as they moved out into the night. The wind had come up in the last couple hours, and as soon as they cleared the door, her husband's floppy jean hat blew off his head. She stood on the sidewalk and waited, a guitar case in each hand, smiling at Lang through the front window, while her husband chased his hat down the street.

By the time Lang got to the Brat and Brau at 10:00, he was drunk. It was a huge place with heavy, darkwood tables spread throughout three rooms. But there were only a few people there, scattered about at tables near the stage. A waitress in jeans and a red and white checkered shirt hustled by him with a wicker bratwurst basket and two glass steins of beer. As Lang headed toward a far corner table, he heard clapping, like tinkling spoons.

She sang like no one he had ever heard, about devils and cheaters and goodtime women who want only to go drinking with the boys. She had changed from jeans into a gray dress that hung all the way to the floor. He sat there drinking his beer slowly, wondering how so much hard music could come out of such a tiny, perfect mouth, imagining her naked body moving like a snake under her long dress, fear and excitement returning, nagging at him like a memory, a vague, flashing memory of fire-fights and ambush patrols.

At break time they headed directly for Lang's table. She sat next to Lang and put her hand on his knee. After the waitress brought their beer, her husband leaned back and spread his legs out in front of him. He still wore his floppy hat. Lang was no longer certain he had ever heard her husband's voice.

Then, after her husband got up to go to the toilet, she leaned over and kissed Lang. He couldn't believe it, but then she kissed him again, and even once more before her husband returned. The second break she kissed him four times, the third break five. At 11:45 she slipped him a napkin with her phone number written on it. Five minutes later he discovered that he was drunk enough to slip her one with his address. At 1:00 he stumbled out into the night air and made his way back to his apartment.

* * *

Lang awoke early and decided that she had been drunk, like him. He had been drunk, God, he had been drunk. So had she. He had to tread more carefully in the future. What the fuck did he think he was doing, anyway?

Fifteen minutes later there was a soft tap on the door. The knock was so soft he waited to hear it again.

He opened the door and there she stood, backpack pulling along the sides of her breasts. Without a word she walked right past him into his bedroom, slipped off her clothes, and slid into his bed. Once he got in with her, she came into his arms and wrapped about him like a spider.

She came every morning and every Saturday afternoon for six months. He completely forgot about his classes and waited only for her arrival. She stayed each weekday morning until 9:30, allowing herself sufficient time to make her 10:00 o'clock music composition class. When the time came to leave, she slipped out of bed quietly as he stretched over onto her side, burrowing his face into her smell; the last sound he heard before falling into a dreamless sleep was her bicycle chain clicking by his bedroom window toward the street.

The second day she sang to him. She crawled out from under the covers, sat naked on her pillow next to his head, and sang "The First Time Ever I Saw Your Face." He had just had his face buried into her long hair, and he could still feel it tingle on his neck and cheek. The room suddenly filled with her smell, and her high forehead and smooth skin drove him crazy. He watched and listened until the last note left her mouth before reaching out and pulling her back into bed.

The third morning she sang to him again, and after she had finished, she asked him to tell about himself. What had he done? Where had he been? Where had he learned to be such a good lover? She snuggled down into the covers, her nose touching his cheek. She caressed his shoulders and looked into his eyes. He felt the warmth of her body next to him, her leg over his hip, and allowed the memories to come flooding back. He began telling her of the war, and once he began, he sang, too, a new language, a language uplifting and inspiring and releasing. That third day he talked and talked on through her class, all the way until noon. And the next morning he anxiously awaited her knock, flat on his back through the whole afternoon and night since she had left the morning before, his fists clenched at his sides, his skin incandescent, stretched so tightly across his skull, he knew he could peel himself with his fingernail. And when her knock came, he cried out and dragged her into bed to begin once again.

She loved to hear him talk about the war, and he loved to hear her sing, but she no longer wanted him to come to their performances, their gigs, as she chose to call them. Her husband, Skip, would be there, and though he knew about her and Lang, naturally—he was a modern, tolerant man, she said, a liberated man, with no controls over her except those she wished to give him—she didn't want them together, anymore. She didn't know why, really.

Lang watched her shake her head. Her hair lay oddly along her right cheek until she shook her head again. She just didn't.

Lang didn't know what she was talking about, but as long as she continued to come every morning and every Saturday afternoon, and as long as she continued to give him his own concert, in the mornings in bed and on Saturday in the living room in front of the television set, he didn't care if he ever left the apartment. And as the days passed he came more and more alive. He told her everything, everything he could think of. He could talk all he wanted, now, he decided; she made him believe he could tell anyone.

But, of course, he should have known that she would never leave her husband, that when her husband, Skip, decided they had to go to Europe because an agent had landed them a full-time, permanent singing job there, she would go with him. Of course. She had to. She *wanted* to. She thought she had made that obvious from the beginning. Hadn't he known that, for God's sake? Well, he should have known.

And one day she was gone and that was that. She didn't come one morning, nor the next, nor the next. Finally, he knew she was gone for good. And he was surprised how quickly and how easily he slipped back into his old life. And how comfortable he was again, and so quickly, too. It was different now, of course, but then, not so different really. After all, he had told no one but her. He had not made that mistake. And she was gone. He didn't have to worry about that. She was gone for good, across the blue water.

Lang immersed himself in his routine and tried not to remember. He even returned to school regularly, though now returning to school was even more like returning to kindergarten. But soon he was thinking about her less and less, and finally, he forced her further and further into his long ago memory, until he nearly forgot her altogether, like he had the war. He once again began buying J&B and watching television alone until late at night. Once more he locked and chained his door and talked to no one. In no time at all he felt good again, he felt comfortable again. How could he have ever been so stupid?

But then one day, three weeks ago, the white postcard came in the mail, intruding from out of the past in a way even the war couldn't. The walls closed in on him, and people on the street looked at him in funny ways. He wandered down Sherman Avenue that first morning and sat out on the pier. After that he began his morning treks, and it seemed as the days passed, that as long as he stayed out on the edge of the blue water day after day, he could keep her away, even though, at night, when he returned to his apartment, the postcard was still there.

* * *

Lang didn't go to the lake that morning. He knew that no amount of staring and hoping along the lake's edge could keep her from his apartment that night at seven o'clock.

He stood in front of a small bar on Johnson Street and looked in through the open doorway. He could see the heads and antlers of caribou on the walls and on the mirror above the bar. He could hear Tammy Wynette cry out to the world's women to stand by their men.

Lang sat on a stool near the door and ordered a beer. He was the only customer, and after serving him, the bartender polished and repolished glasses with a white towel at the other end of the bar. Lang finished his beer quickly and ordered another. He placed his feet on the metal rest at the bottom of the stool next to him. The bartender refilled Lang's glass, then returned to his place, polishing a single glass over and over. Swizzle sticks with caribou antler tips stuck out of containers above the bar. Lang reached for a bowl of popcorn just as Judy Collins told him she'd be going with him someday soon.

A half hour later a woman walked in and sat two stools down. She ordered a whiskey-seven and nodded a toast to Lang as she brought the glass to her lips. She smiled at him.

Lang finished his beer and placed his glass firmly on the bar— as if he had finally decided something once and for all. The woman got up and moved down to the seat next to him. She put her hand on his arm and drank with her other hand, motioning for two more. She looked up at Lang, and he stared into her blue eyes.

"My mother is a drug addict," she said, "and my father raped me when I was ten years old."

She shifted in her seat and moved in even closer, her head bent toward him. The bartender stopped polishing and turned, waiting, listening, his mouth open.

"In the Ia-Drang Valley," Lang began, "The Vietcong came thundering out of the horizon like buffalo, and the rounds blew by my ears like snow in a whistling wind."

WHEN ONLY TOO LONG
IS LONG ENOUGH

BY THE TIME Hackett met Thuy, he'd already settled into his routine. He had two jobs in the Order of Battle section of the MACV compound. In the morning he was a document filer. He filed captured documents by unit into manila folders, and since the documents were often bloody and musty and stunk of gunpowder and sour rotting flesh, sealed them airtight into steel-gray, metal safes. In the afternoon he was a map pinner. He stuck blue pins into one of the giant green maps of Vietnam on the wall of the O.B. section.

It didn't take him long at all to settle in. In the morning he splashed on so much after shave and cologne that it nearly covered the smell. And he passed the long afternoons by daydreaming of taking life into his own hands. He dreamed of God and moving pins around, removing pins, or adding more, depending on his mood.

He'd also gotten himself a room in Saigon to escape the green and tan boredom of Tan-Son-Nhut Airbase. It was on the seventh floor of a building on a dead end road off of Truong-Minh-Ky, a building set out alone in the middle of a field. The room had a refrigerator, a tiny sink, a table, a chair, and a double bed. It also had a toilet with a door that didn't close. And from the small balcony he could look out over Truong-Minh-Ky and northwestern Saigon. It cost outrageously, but he had nothing to save his money for.

At night, after work, Hackett hit the bars along Truong-Minh-Ky, drank *Ba-Muoi-Ba,* and whored until he was exhausted enough to fall into his seventh floor double bed. At 7:00 A.M. a *xich-lo* took him to MACV, to more bloody documents and more bombing pins.

Then one morning, out of the blue, she appeared as the new MACV Snack Bar cashier.

He rolled his tray of gray, runny chop suey along the shiny metal bars to the register. When he looked up to pay, there she was, batting her eyes at him from out of the thickest black hair he'd ever seen. He grinned a silly grin and bent his shoulders inward, trying to collapse inside himself. She smiled indulgently and gave him his change.

From that first day Hackett began living with a new excitement. The blood and flesh smelled better, he daydreamed less, took more care with the pins, the whores were more fun, and the *Ba-Muoi-Ba* tasted less like formaldehyde. He even found a floor-length bamboo curtain to replace his toilet door.

His fifth time through the snack bar line, he mustered enough nerve to ask her her name. He spoke in halting, pidgin English, and she chided him for not speaking correctly. She could understand him very well if he spoke proper English, she said. Her name was Thuy. He stumbled to a white formica table to stare at her until his food was cold and his lunch break was over.

From there they moved on to a few more words and then a few more, until eventually, she accepted an invitation to take her break with him. Soon after, it was lunch, and finally, one night, she offered him a ride home on her terrible green Honda.

She drove like a maniac, and as they blew down Truong-Minh-Ky, he clung to her, hugging her back and smelling her skin of Ivory Soap, her thick black hair tickling his cheeks like bird wings. He was terrified out of his mind, but he wanted the ride to go on forever, the city sliding by like a piece of cardboard.

Soon she was taking him home every night.

She studied English at one of the many English schools that had sprung up all over Saigon after the American occupation had begun. She worked at her English tirelessly and was proud of her ability. She read American novels voraciously—anything she could get her hands on. She raved on and on to him about authors he'd never heard of above the din of the motorcycle and the clatter of the Saigon streets. He tried his best to listen to every-thing she said, though he was often stunned and frightened by her sharp mind. But she suffered his ignorance willingly, rolling her eyes and smiling.

He wooed her tentatively, knowing he had to watch his step with a woman like her—someone who wasn't a whore or bargirl, someone he couldn't just reach out and grab simply because he wanted to. Finally, one night, before they boarded her Honda, she asked him to come home with her to dinner. Her parents had left for the evening, she said, and she wanted to cook him a real Viet-namese meal.

After dinner they sat on the davenport. In time he reached over and kissed her. Soon they were locked into an embrace, and he had what he'd wanted for five months, right there on the daven-port. They even fell asleep for an hour in each other's arms so he had to rush out the door before her parents returned.

After that she came to his room every night and stayed with him for a couple of hours before she had to go home for dinner. They lounged in bed and giggled, or he kneeled naked over his Sterno can stove, cooking himself Campbell's Pork and Beans or spaghetti and meat balls, while she lay in bed, a sheet snuggled around her neck. Later, wearing black silk robes with orange but-terflies that she'd bought for them on the black market, they looked out over Saigon from his tiny balcony.

After she left, he either went to Truong-Minh-Ky for a few beers or stayed in his room and tried to catch up on some of those writers he'd missed. Then he slept the blissful sleep of one con-tent with the world and his life. And at 7:00 A.M. he rode a *xich-lo* to work, anticipating the same thing all over again.

* * *

But then, with only two months left on his tour, the embarrassing questions began. What were they going to do now? she asked, as they both lay in bed staring at the ceiling. He only had two months left, after all. Did he want her to return to America with him, or would he return to Saigon as a civilian? What kind of job would he get? When would they get married?

Hackett rolled over and looked at the wall in front of his bal-cony. Wallpaper tigers suddenly twisted into slaughtered lambs. He'd never considered the consequences. He was happy with her, it passed the time, and he loved her, sure, but he loved her here, for now. Saigon wasn't the world. The world was different. Once he got back, the world would change everything.

He rolled over to her and took her hand. She pulled her thigh up over his leg. Yes, he'd take her with him. Yes, they'd go to America together, get married, and settle down. He'd work for the government. There would be no problem, no problem at all. But first he'd have to extend his tour six months so he could complete all the paperwork. Or if she wanted, they could come back together after they were married, and he'd teach at one of the English schools. It was up to her. It didn't really matter to him, as long as they remained together.

So he never did anything, except creep away without her like a sneak in the night after his two months were up. And she never suspected a thing. She remained innocent until the morning he left. And once he was on the plane, he knew that he'd done the right thing, that she'd have no trouble getting over it. She'd be all right, too, he knew. She'd have no problem forgetting him, either. She could take care of herself. And after he and his group landed in California, he celebrated like all the others by screaming and dancing and kissing American soil.

But he'd miscalculated and been wrong about forgetting. Once he got home, obsession crept up his spine and his conscience refused to allow him any rest. Guilt thickened his life and voices drummed in his head. He'd tricked her; he'd abandoned her without explanation. He'd used her and now she was probably dead and he'd killed her. And even if he was lucky and could turn off the guilt for a brief time, there were always the dreams that came on him like a roller coaster in the night, every night. And the intensity of the dreams never flagged, ever.

He dreamed of her in huge sunglasses, whizzing down Truong-Minh-Ky on her green Honda, weaving between *xich-los*, jeeps, cabs, and trucks, displaying just enough smooth, brown thigh to drive the traditional Vietnamese crazy, her thick black hair straight behind like a raven in mid-flight, as if the faster she went, the farther from Saigon she would become . . . and then her motorcycle blown skyhigh in slow motion, spots of her blood and bits of her flesh spattering his face and arms . . . or she floated alone in a rickety sampan, her black hair wild and straight in the air like branches from a leafless tree, accusing him over and over of crime after crime . . . or she was on her knees begging piasters in a Saigon street, her face a chunk of deformed, knarred flesh . . .

And then there was the television. Once the fatal communist advance and the government collapse became imminent, he watched every news program available on his set, all day and all evening long. He even set his alarm clock to wake him out of his dreams in order to catch some late-night or early-morning newscast. He watched transfixed as news reports rolled forth, news reports of blood and guts and cowardly ARVNs. He watched reporters barely able to hide their glee (See what is happening? We always told you so!). And as the advance moved ever onward toward Saigon itself, Hackett looked for Thuy among the people fleeing in *xich-los,* cars, and on foot. And finally, as the attack on Saigon began, he was positive he saw her hanging onto a helicopter rudder, flying through the air until she could hang on no longer and fell out of camera range.

So she was dead for sure, or if not dead, in a stern communist re-education camp, bending her lovely back over some dusty construction project, sweat rolling off her beautiful neck, damp strands of black hair clinging to her cheeks, falling exhausted into a hard cot in a sterile barracks with fifty others.

* * *

Then one day, out of the blue, a letter came.

John Hammer. He'd been a map pinner, too, though a thoroughly dedicated one. He pinned enemy KIA results, and Hackett often watched Hammer slide a pin in slowly and deliberately, then remove his hand for another. Hackett ignored him as best he could, but naturally Hammer knew about Thuy. He enjoyed teasing Hackett about Thuy nearly as much as he enjoyed pinning maps. It was the usual kind of casual thing—How's your gook today, gooklover? When you getting married? Where you gonna settle down, gooklover? At home with dear old mom and dad?

And of course Hackett had let it pass. Once he met Thuy, he ignored most everything but her. He just let the time slide by until it was over and he boarded his Freedom Bird.

But now, out of the blue, he had a letter from Hammer.

He'd seen her, he said, his gook, Thuy. She was living in New York, in Rochester. He'd seen her on the street, out of the blue, he said. And it was her, all right, no mistake. He couldn't resist letting Hackett know. He found his address through an old army buddy. Hammer even supplied Thuy's address at the bottom. He somehow found that through some army buddy, too.

After the shock, Hackett read the letter again, thrilled and appalled at what he knew she must have endured. He could see her clutching to the edge of a rocking sampan, riding the waves of the South China Sea with too many others, stuffed and squeezed, some already dead and bloated, floating in the sea around them, the stench attracting circling birds . . . and then rescued, emaciated, scarred in body and mind, kissing the feet of her saviors . . . and now the poverty of America.

He'd have to search her out. He had no money, but that wasn't a problem. He could hitchhike; he didn't have a job, either. He packed a knapsack and set out that minute. There was no reason to waste time.

He found her address with little trouble. It was on East Avenue, a lovely tree-lined street, a fashionable street for those who were still willing to live downtown. He stood in front of the plush building and checked the address again. The gabled tower rose twenty stories.

In the lobby there was an elegantly lettered sign next to her mailbox:

Thuy Vertel
Exclusive Interior Design
Call for appointment
(716) 763-8102

Hackett knew he had no right, but he rang the bell nonetheless. He shook his head and waited.

She opened the door part way, without unlatching the chain, and he looked in at her. Her hair was short and curled all over. She wore designer jeans and a T-shirt with the golden locks of Peter Frampton splayed across her breasts.

"I'm sorry," he muttered. "I'm Jim."

"Oh?" she asked, holding her head high, looking him up and down. She made no move to remove the chain. "And do I know you?"

"Jim. Jim Hackett. You remember. Vietnam. Saigon."

"Oh, yes, Jim." Her eyes clouded over. She removed the chain. "How are you, Jim? Won't you come in?"

He sat on a davenport, and she sat across from him on a chair. The davenport was so soft that he felt two feet tall. Her chair was huge, high, and straight-backed, like a throne. He hollered up at her.

"How are you, Thuy?"

"I'm fine," she said. She paused. "Jim?" she asked.

He stared at Peter Frampton. A breeze billowed black robes with orange butterflies.

"I shouldn't have come."

He crawled out of the davenport and headed fast for the door. She called after him.

"I'm sorry. It was a very long time ago."

"Yes," he said and closed the door. "A very long time ago."

ASYLUM

THE ASYLUM WAS in the most hotly contested area of Bien-Hoa Province, near the tiny hamlet of Tam-Hiep—a few, dusty, isolated weed huts along the muddy banks of the Bien-Hoa River. The asylum was three hundred yards away from the village, surrounded by a high cement fence topped with embedded broken glass, to keep the insane in and the evil spirits from drifting over to contaminate the village. The Vietnamese traditionally considered insanity catching.

Since the insane were locked in and no one wished to be contaminated, the patients were left to fend for themselves. There were no attendants. The courtyard of the asylum was piled with bones, discarded paper, feces, and busy rats.

Once a day, in the early morning, their food was brought by an old man from the village in a creaky water buffalo cart. He placed the day's rations on a squat table just inside the gate, and left again until the next morning. There would be a cauldron of rice, a pot of meat, ten large French loaves, three packs of Park Lane cigarettes, and two small boxes of matches.

When the Fifth Infantry broke through to the village and entered the asylum grounds, they were appalled by what they saw. They stared with drooping mouths at the incredible filth. They couldn't believe it.

Then something drew them to it. They dropped their weapons

and other gear at their sides and went to work. They didn't hesitate; they dug right in.

They opened the doors and windows and drove out all the rats. They buried and burned all the garbage. They brought out paint, boards, and nails, and all the other equipment they had lugged along for the pacification of the village.

All the villagers from Tam-Hiep came out and looked on, amazed once again at the strange things appearing before their eyes. They watched the men work all day and on into the evening. They took a spontaneous holiday. They watched as the infantrymen fed those who had difficulty feeding themselves. They watched giant, battle-hardened soldiers take grown Vietnamese men and women onto their laps and delicately feed them with their messkit spoons. They watched them fix and paint and clean. They watched them and smiled. They shook their heads.

Once it grew dark, the men set up camp on the asylum courtyard grounds. They pitched tents, cut trenches, and ate C-Rations and leftovers. The villagers returned to their weed huts for their own meals. As they squatted around their rice pots and shoveled in from their bowls, they chatted noisily. They grinned and smiled and laughed often. These Americans. They shook their heads over and over. Strange people, these Americans.

Later, after the men of the Fifth Infantry finished eating and smoking, for a little relaxation and amusement, and to relieve the tension they had been under, they raped and killed all the villagers. Then they burned the village down.

At dawn, they broke camp and left. The insane waved goodbye from the courtyard gate, and the men waved back. The village still smoldered as the men fanned out into the black-green jungle and disappeared. The insane ambled happily back into the asylum and went about the business of being insane.

THURSDAYS

ON THURSDAYS IN Detroit three-hundred-pound Arabs in dark shades sit on their porches eating sweets and drinking dark green tea from tall glasses, shotguns next to their chairs, sabers in their silk sashes, while John sits in the dark in his living room across the street, his M-16 upon his thighs, watching "The Guiding Light." Sometimes the Arabs wave at John when they catch a glimpse of him in the moonlight through his dark window, as he moves down the hall with his M-16 to the toilet or to the kitchen for a sandwich. Or sometimes, on other days, when they see him come along the street from work, they laugh and wave, crying out to him, making guttural, barking noises in their language that sounds like no other, as if they are on the verge of throwing up. John knows they have a reputation as killers, these Arabs, as violent, dark-eyed men who will kill quickly, without reason, pounce on anyone with their sabers or blast anyone's belly open with their shotguns, just for the pleasure of feeding their passion for blood. And sometimes John even goes to his living room window and opens it enough to hear them laugh and talk. Sometimes he stands at the window long enough to see them slap each other's large thighs and broad backs, their beards waving like dirty rags.

John watches Ed Bauer, his favorite character from "The Guiding Light," suddenly lash out at his wife, Mo, and realizes with great insight that Ed has changed a good deal in the last few years: He is less likely now to whimper and sigh before impossible problems, less long-suffering, more willing to rage at the overwhelming odds loose in the world.

Heather the Whore lives in the apartment upstairs from John. When Heather first moved in, only a week after John himself moved in, eight days after he had returned from Vietnam, he met her on the steps on his way in from the corner grocery store. Heather the Whore smiled and said hello that fine morning, so moving him by her friendliness, that he smiled back into her young, blonde face and invited her inside for a beer. Later, after they had talked for some time about how strange it was to live in a neighborhood filled with bearded, armed Arabs in dark glasses, and how strange it was, too, that the police never seemed to even come near this part of town, and had downed three or four beers apiece, something heavy and unusual moved in John's chest, choking off his breath like a chunk of moss. He leaned over on his new sofa and asked her shyly if he could kiss her. But as soon as he had spoken, Heather the Whore laughed uproariously, slapping her smooth, bare thigh in time to her gasping, sobbing laughter. And after she had finally gotten control of herself and handed him her glass, she rose, called him Loverboy, and sashayed her gorgeous hips out the front door.

Later in the day George the Pimp took John aside and set him straight. George is a white giant whose huge feet pound the stairs to Heather's apartment day and night, again and again, until he seems about to break through and tumble into John's place below. John remembers the day George set him straight better than he remembers anything else, even war. He and George stood next to each other on the front porch like old friends, George with one of his giant hands on John's left shoulder, squeezing. Heather was a whore, see, and what's more, she was his whore and she didn't do anything without his say so, not even fart, understand? George smiled menacingly and squeezed harder. John was close enough to see the appalling pock marks in George the Pimp's corrupt face. The sky was bright blue, and the sun hung over the tall pine tree in the front yard. Across the street one Arab slapped another good-naturedly on the back and drank from a steaming glass of tea.

And Heather hasn't been able to stop laughing at John for all these years. Whenever they meet on the porch, she laughs through painted red lips and calls him Sweetie and Bigboy and Lover as he pushes past her into his apartment. She is still a slight, honey blonde, still in great demand in her profession. All night John hears George the Pimp's pounding footsteps, Heather's clients following timidly on the stairs behind, as if they're afraid they'll wake a sleeping child, the bed squeaking, squeaking, squeaking. Sometimes John is amazed that Heather looks as good as she does, even now; but then she has not lived a hard life, he tells himself over and over, day in and day out. He would still give anything to kiss her.

* * *

Heather the Whore and her Chinese friends, Chinh and Lanh, two other whores, have parties every Thursday night. John watches Asians of all kinds follow Heather and her friends up the steps to Heather's apartment, young yellow men in tuxedos and women in elaborate evening gowns, carrying cases and baskets filled with crab and caviar, liver pâté and champagne. The party goes on all night—footfalls on John's ceiling, Asian voices filtering down, music rattling the walls.

One evening years ago, when Heather had her first party, John was struck numb as he watched all those Asians head up Heather's stairs, their Asian voices and Asian languages finding him through the ceiling above. The walls closed around his head, and he began flashing back: He heard scratching on the outside walls of the house like cat claws. He looked out the window and saw Asians dancing out on the lawn, surrounding the house, fires burning about them, the night bright in their eyes. The night turned hot, a stifling wind began blowing, drying the inside of his mouth. He stripped off his shirt and stalked from room to room, his M-16 at port arms, Asian eyes following him through the windows, sweat beading on his back and chest.

Finally, later, after his fear had eased and he could no longer see them out on the lawn, no longer hear claws scratching the walls, he painted his face and chest black, slapped a starlight scope onto his M-16, went out into the back yard and sat on the lawn near the garage, sighting their shadows through Heather's upstairs window. He planned to stay out there until daybreak or until someone made a move for him. But as the night wore on, the party merely grew wilder: Asians began coming out Heather's upstairs window to stand on the ledge and urinate off the roof, screaming and crying out into the night. Eventually, John got up and headed back inside. He had been mistaken; it was just another party: they were only drunk and drugged and harmless. So now when Heather the Whore and her Chinese friends, Chinh and Lanh, have a party, John just dozes in his chair most of the night, his M-16 across his knees, caressing the trigger.

* * *

Thursdays are John's only days off. Six days a week, including Sundays, he drives a minibus filled with severely retarded adults about the city of Detroit. He is supposed to lead them on trips to zoos and outings to museums and public buildings, display them before the community as model, tax dollar beneficiaries. John doesn't do what his job description requires of him, however. Instead, every morning except Thursday, at 7:00 A.M., after they leave the retarded shelter garage, he fills the bus gas tank, using money from his own pocket, and drives the retarded throughout the city until 5:30, talking continuously about Vietnam as he drives.

He talks as Jane, the one who loves him, crawls up behind his seat and hugs him as tightly as she can, her lips protruding like a dead carp's. Throughout the day, as Jane hugs and drools, John tells of some long-forgotten terror, some long-lost horror. He prattles on and on about Vietnam; he never tires, talking as if they listen, as if they follow what he says. As the Bagman paces the aisle, all his belongings in the two paper bags he clutches at his sides, John drives about the streets of Detroit, braking for traffic and stopping for lights. As he drives he tells them about the night on ambush when he opened fire a split-second too soon, just as his best friend leaped into the air in front of him for no reason at all. John was absolutely sure he had cut his friend down. He was horrified and knew at once he'd never get over it—he could see the rest of his life, days upon days, as a suffering, miserable wretch—until his friend sat up and turned to him grinning, flashing absurd white teeth. John had never seen such an absurd grin in such an absurd place. And John tells the retarded how he lost control and laughed out in the dark jungle night until, later on, the rest of the patrol had to hold him down and cover his mouth before he got them all killed.

So as Stella picks her teeth and her lover, Ralph, watches her longingly, as if he is trying to find a way inside to help her, John tells them about the vision that changed his life forever. While Terrible Tom shakes his fist and threatens violence on them all, even those he sees passing out the bus window, his huge head moving from side to side, John tells them about the day he was driving alone down Highway One between Hue and Da Nang, when he saw a man, his wife, and their four young sons in a paddy alongside the road, all with their backs bent, hands thrust into the water. As John passed in his jeep, he thought absently how lucky this family was to have so many sons to work the field, when suddenly they all rose in unison and began waving their hands madly, twisting their mouths into odd shapes, screwing up their eyes, making hideous faces. John tells the retarded how he knew then and there that the family was trying to warn him of unbearable things to come, so he did the only thing he could do; he changed his insides with drugs. He tells them, too, how once he started he couldn't stop, but smoked, ate, and poked needles until everything was gone completely, until everything disappeared.

* * *

It is late in the evening, and the soap operas are all over for another Thursday. John watches a blank television screen and chews dryly on another peanut butter sandwich. Crumbs cling to him, and he can hear Arabs through an open window, talking and laughing and drinking tea out on their porches up and down the street, even at this late hour. The Arabs with their guns and swords, their reputation and their late hours have made his neighborhood the safest in Detroit: The usual crimes—burglary, murder, rape, theft—so rampant everywhere else in the city, are non-existent here.

But John knows that this night is strange: Heather's party has ended early—the music has ceased and the voices have stopped filtering down. The bed, however, begins to squeak upstairs, and John wonders vaguely if the Asian men are lining up for Heather the Whore and her Chinese whore friends, Chinh and Lanh, while the other Asian women look on, still in their lovely evening gowns, stuffed with champagne and caviar. The squeaking stops and starts again and again as the minutes pass, and John realizes that he is right.

Music wafts across the night from somewhere, from someone else's house far down the street perhaps. It is Shelley Fabares singing "Johnny Angel," and John listens closely, until he hears her telling him over and over that he is an angel to her. The minutes begin passing in jerks and jumps, like rounds squeezed off slowly and methodically, until John is on his feet, his M-16 cradled like an infant in his arms, as he listens to the bed squeak louder and louder, wailing like a scream for help. Then, putting his fingers to his lips, he knows that it is no longer the bed squeaking, but the sound coming from his own mouth.

THE CHANCE ENCOUNTER OF HABERMANN THE TRANSLATOR AND LY THE STREET URCHIN AND HOW THEIR LIVES ARE CHANGED FOREVER

HER MOTHER AND father were dead, so she slept in an alley behind a BOQ hotel on Tran-Hung-Dao Street at the edge of Cholon. And every morning for four months when he left in a motorized *xich-lo* for his job at MACV as a Vietnamese translator, Habermann saw her standing just outside the hotel sand drum barricade. And every evening, too, after refusing his *xich-lo* driver's offers of the pleasures of drugs and the sexual charms of his twelve-year-old cousin, and after paying the driver what he deserved rather than what he demanded, then walking away from his driver's complaining harangue toward the hotel, Habermann saw her again, exactly as he had seen her in the morning, two stuffed paper bags at her sides, her long black hair swept from her eyes like perfection, oblivious to the amazing activity about her, as if she were somehow frozen solid with heat, smiling a forlorn, world-weary smile, but smiling nonetheless, like the world was a place where everything was as it should be and it was her duty to endure, a little girl without parents in the midst of a war without end.

But one evening after four months, for no reason other than the evening was unusually cool and the prospect of another three hours among squealing, jaded bargirls was so repulsive that he knew if he stepped one foot toward downtown, he would suddenly run howling through the streets to join the mad, the demented, the twisted of the world, he stopped and asked her her name. Her name was Ly, and they talked for three hours, until curfew forced him back to his hotel room, about her dead mother and father and her only living family member, her thirteen-year-old brother who took care of her, the noise of Tran-Hung-Dao Street converging and abating by turn, until he knew he would no longer care about the bars for the rest of his life.

What was his name? she wanted to know. His name was Habermann, he said, but his Vietnamese teachers in America had called him Hai, and he liked to be called by that name best. He worked on the edge of Saigon, on the big air base called Tan-Son-Nhut.

Yes, she knew where Tan-Son-Nhut was. Before her parents were killed in a mortar attack two years ago, they all lived on a street next to the main gate. Her father had been in the air force, she said, dropping her hands from her bags and tilting her head, lightly stroking her hair. A major.

Then, without thinking, Habermann told her a joke he had overheard another translator tell a bargirl his first evening downtown four months ago, a joke Habermann had since told over and over, night after night.

The reason he spoke Vietnamese so well, he said, was because he was actually Vietnamese, but some terrible mistake had occurred. He had somehow been born in America to the wrong woman. He was here to find the American, his brother, who had been born out of the wrong woman's body in Vietnam, so they could finally make the switch, so they could straighten things out for good.

Habermann laughed as he finished, but Ly only smiled weakly and clutched at her bags again. Habermann leaned against the sand drum and looked out at the street. What the hell did you say to children, anyway? He felt his face get hot and sweat tingle his back.

A few feet in front of them a sandwich vendor made a French loaf sandwich for a customer. He sliced the green peppers and tomatoes carefully, meticulously, and placed them and the strips of gray meat onto the split loaf before dousing it with *nuoc-mam* from a plastic ketchup dispenser. Finally, he wrapped the sandwich in newspaper and handed it across the counter. The billboard above the movie theatre across the street advertised another swashbuckler, the two brilliantly painted stars staring out at the street below through ambiguously shaped eyes. Eventually, Habermann turned to Ly again.

What was she doing out here, anyway? he wanted to know. He saw her in the same spot morning and night, he said. And how old was she and why wasn't she in school?

She was eight, she said, and she waited here every day for her brother. She didn't know what her brother did, only that he went out early and returned late with a little money for them, enough for food. She didn't care what he did, she said, her eyes downcast, her smile gone for the moment, as if she knew that what her brother did was something unmentionable, something so unbearably corrupt, even here, that she had to keep it from one such as he, an American like all Americans, always searching for the innocent, the naive, even here. But Habermann did imagine a male facsimile of her; perhaps he had even seen her brother, pimping in the Rose, the New York, the Elysee, spewing Yankee slang from a child's mouth.

"You fuck, GI? You want girl? My sister good girl. She fuck you, GI."

Ly kept track of their clothes, she said, their possessions. She pulled her bags even closer now and held on. Rice pots, chopsticks, and clothes stuck out of the two paper bags. That was her job, she said.

Habermann looked at her closely, smiling again like she smiled every morning and every evening. He could see she was determined. Everything was fine, just fine.

Yes, he said, he could see that.

* * *

As the days passed into weeks, Habermann found himself becoming obsessed with Ly. He couldn't explain his obsession—it surprised and confused him but he simply accepted it, like he accepted the necessity of spending his twenty-sixth year in a war without end. In the evening he watched for her as he came down the street in his *xich-lo*, once the hotel came into sight, as if a glorious fantasy, a renewal of some kind were about to appear, corruption and evil pushed back into the noise of the street. Sometimes his ears rang as he neared the hotel. Sometimes he couldn't hear at all until her cry of greeting.

As he worked during the day, he thought about her, standing in the street, on her own staked-out corner, willing to protect her paper bags with everything her fragile young life possessed. He could barely wait for the work day to be over so he could get back to her. He even began neglecting his job—reams of documents, transcripts from Radio Hanoi broadcasts of running dogs and lackeys, South Vietnamese Puppets and American Imperialists—stacked on his desk in front of his daydreaming eyes, until a superior finally prodded him to a quick burst of work. Habermann and Ly talked every night until the last minute before 11:00 P.M. curfew.

As the MP guarded the hotel from his kiosk, his shiny, black helmet reflecting the lights of the street, Habermann talked to Ly about his life in America, his wife, and all the plans they had after the war. And Ly seemed to understand so well. She asked questions, the right questions. She asked him about his wife, his parents, about America.

* * *

He and his wife both grew up in southern Minnesota as childhood sweethearts. They were both only children, and their parents had amazingly all dropped dead within four months of each other, his mother and her father from cancer, and his father and her mother of heart failure. This weird quirk of life tightened their bond, these family deaths bringing them even closer together.

After high school he continued to work in the grocery store, and she worked as a bank clerk. She had been left a modest house on Elm Street, and they were both extremely frugal—they went out little and saved their money. Where this penchant for frugality came from he had no idea: their parents had been generous, as generous as their working-class means allowed. But there it was nonetheless.

They set a seven-year goal, a seven-year plan (they decided to live the rest of their lives in seven-year installments), then marriage and travel. They were both crazy about travel. They wanted to go everywhere—Europe, Australia, South America, Asia. They weren't interested in college, and children weren't a part of their plans, either. Neither had ever wanted any. It had been another thing which had drawn them together.

But the sixth year of their first seven-year plan, Vietnam blackened the horizon and thrust their lives into the unknown. They tried to do their best to deal with it. They decided to get married at once. They also decided that he should enlist to stay out of the war—an army recruiter told them that if Habermann enlisted, because of his high test scores, he would go to OCS and then to language school. Then at least they could be together somewhere. Germany maybe. Or even Turkey. But one of the ironies of the war met them almost at once: after OCS he was sent to *Vietnamese* language school.

* * *

As time passed Habermann brought Ly presents to make her happy, to light up her face. Every night now he got out of his *xich-lo* laden with gifts: bright colored movie magazines (for which she was insatiable), candy bars from the MACV PX, cellophane bags of French candy from the black market vendors on Le-Loi, and two red cartons of Marlboros for her brother. He had no clear idea what was happening, what was moving him to such lengths, only that he was moving and that there was nothing he could do; answers of any kind were beyond him.

He took hundreds of pictures of her with his Polaroid camera; she was also insatiable for pictures. He asked passersby—*xich-lo* drivers, whores, pimps, street vendors, GIs, communists, probably—to take pictures of them in different poses. They spent hours pouring over their pictures; sometimes they giggled over the absurdity of their expressions; other times they commented quite seriously about making them better the next time.

Then one evening, after convincing Ly that they could take her bags with them—Habermann carrying one, she the other—and return in plenty of time before curfew and her appointment with her brother, they walked to the Thanh-Bich Restaurant for dinner. The restaurant was just off the major traffic circle where Tran-Hung-Dao and Le-Loi met, the juncture between Chinese Cholon and downtown Saigon, and they walked the fifteen blocks slowly, wedging through crowds, struggling with their bags, dodging motorbikes, jeeps, trucks, taxicabs, and *xich-los* at every turn and every crosswalk. Habermann kept hold of Ly's hand to keep her from being swallowed up. As they walked he realized that this was the first time he had touched her.

A few sidewalk tables were spread out in front of the doorway of the restaurant, but Habermann and Ly took one where Ly wanted, inside, along the right wall, across the room from the ice cream counter. From where Habermann sat, he could watch the traffic on Le-Loi and the waiters hurrying from table to table, in and out the door.

They shoveled the food into their mouths from the plates and bowls placed before them—the restaurant speciality, a large dish of *com be tet*, brown fried rice and a small piece of steak with a large egg over the top, mixed vegetable dishes, a bowl of greens, and *nuoc-mam* fish sauce to drench everything. Habermann ordered a *Ba-Muoi-Ba* for himself and a Coke for Ly.

Maybe her brother could join them here later in the week, he said, sipping his beer. She could ask him tonight and then let Habermann know tomorrow.

No, she said at once, without looking up from her food. Her brother detested Americans. He hated her seeing Habermann, even. They argued about it every night.

She looked up finally and smiled through a mouth filled with rice and egg. But he smoked the cigarettes, she said.

Habermann drank more beer and watched her eat. Jesus, he couldn't imagine what he would do, if he couldn't see her any more.

Ly looked up again. Don't worry, she said, swallowing, she didn't let her brother tell her who she could talk to. Habermann should just keep bringing the cigarettes.

An argument began outside in front of the open doorway between a *xich-lo* driver and a GI. Vietnamese street people and merchants crowded around. "You pay, GI." "Fuck you, man. I'll fuckin' blow you away, man." Habermann heard spectators murmuring, sneering, *thang-meo, thang-meo, thang-meo*.

Ly was still eating, but her Coke was gone. Habermann ordered her another and another *Ba-Muoi-Ba* for himself. He watched Ly, pouring her Coke into her glass, and asked her suddenly if she could read.

Could she read? Of course she could read. And she began reading signs on the walls of the restaurant and outside into the street. Ice Cream 80p. Bicycle and Motorcycle Repairs. Magazines, Cigarettes, Tobacco. Keep Right. Two Wheel Parking Only. She picked up the menu card. Rice, beefsteak, and egg. Tea, milk,

Coca-Cola. Hadn't she read the menu when they ordered? Her brother taught her new words every night.

Okay, okay, Habermann said. She could read. Okay, fine. But what about school? Wouldn't she like to go to school?

Her eyes lit briefly, but died by the time she put down her chopsticks and bowl. She said no. She could read better every day. That was enough.

But was she happy? he insisted.

Ly stared, her hands on the table, her brow furrowed, like she was awaiting instructions. Happy. She said it again, like it was a new word her brother had just taught her, perhaps even a word from another language. She said it once more, then picked up her bowl and chopsticks and continued eating.

Habermann heard a mortar explode close by, down the street a ways, toward Cholon, and thought briefly about going to the doorway to investigate but changed his mind. Ly had finally finished everything, including her Coke. He asked her if she wanted some ice cream.

* * *

The Thanh-Bich became their favorite place, and every night, after he met her, loaded with gifts, they stuffed the candy, magazines, and cigarettes into her bags and off they went, dragging the bags the fifteen blocks to the restaurant, holding hands. And later, after dinner, they made the trek home again and talked in front of the barricade until curfew.

But then one day from out of nowhere at all, Habermann received orders to be transferred to Nha-Trang for the duration of his tour. He waited two more days, until the night before he was to leave, to tell Ly.

After they finished eating and he was drinking his fourth beer and Ly her third Coke, he blurted it out, without preliminaries. She knew how the army was, he said, the war. Her dad had been in the air force. Habermann had no choice, he told her; he had to go. But he would return and see her again before he left Vietnam. He would have a week in Saigon in August, before he was to fly home.

But Ly said no, he wouldn't come back. She'd never see him again. She knew better than that. They should say good-bye now, forever. And it was okay, she said. She knew this day would come.

She sat very straight in her chair, so grown up, he thought. He finished his beer and pushed his glass away.

But he shouldn't lie to her, Ly continued. He shouldn't say he was coming back. She had tears in her eyes but her voice didn't break. She wanted to go now, she said. She was finished with her Coke.

Habermann didn't push it; he let her have her way. He said good-bye at curfew and squeezed her shoulder, but she pulled back and looked the other way. Well, he knew that he would see her again, when he got back to Saigon in August. This wasn't good-bye, no matter what she thought; he knew better than that. He'd still have a chance to say good-bye.

So the next morning as he rode away in his *xich-lo* toward MACV for the last time, he saw her waiting as she always had been, waiting for her brother, for the day to end and for another to follow—perhaps even for the war to end—but no longer waiting for him.

* * *

Once Habermann got to Nha-Trang, once he was apart from Ly and knew he would not see her again until August, he fantasized about her as his own child. While he worked at his new job translating captured documents in his air-conditioned Quonset hut on the edge of the air base, alone with a brown, bare, wooden table and a coffee cup, B-52s and F-105s overhead rattling the walls, documents sometimes too blood soaked to translate, love letters and poems sometimes too heart-rending and personal for any war effort, he saw her with them in their house on Elm Street, going off to school every day, wearing pink party dresses on special occasions—her first dance. He saw himself taking her to breakfast on Saturday mornings at the local diner, teaching her to enjoy greasy eggs and sausage. He saw her on her first real date, he and her mother fretting for her safety and for their own hearts, even wanting to follow the young lovers off in their car to make sure. And he saw her go off to college and become a famous surgeon, later treating her mother and father's ailments lovingly and with patience. And he even saw his grandchildren poking about his feet in his venerable old age.

Within a week after his arrival at Nha-Trang, Habermann knew he had to write his wife and tell her all, no matter how she responded, no matter what she thought. He had to take the chance. He was afraid of what she might say—all their plans, all these years—but he knew there was no turning back. After a month he mailed her a very carefully composed letter.

There was this little girl he had met, a street urchin, no parents, just a thirteen-year-old brother to take care of her. And lo and behold he had gone crazy for her, and all he could think of now was her as their child. He wanted to adopt her. Could she imagine? *Him* wanting a child? He had no idea himself why the big change, but there it was. And he couldn't help himself. Could she find it in her heart to change her mind? He knew how much it was to ask, but he had to ask it. Could she? He could even send her a picture.

In her letter his wife admitted to always having wanted a child. It had been her secret. But now. She didn't even want to see a picture, she said. She'd be crazy about her, she knew, no matter what. He should just bring her home. He shouldn't worry, not a bit. She could hardly wait to see her, to meet her, to hold her in her arms, to see them all together. Just bring her home. She could barely wait.

Habermann slept very little those last three months. He began paperwork with the army and the Vietnamese government. He even got forms for a month's emergency extension of his tour if it turned out that he needed it. After his wife's letter, he moved from place to place, from office to office, bribe to bribe, like one demented, obsessed. Just bring her home. She could barely wait. As he moved through the camp day after day, he already saw Ly's face when he told her, blissful, *happy*.

* * *

He returns to Saigon in August just as he promised, but she no longer stands clutching her bags alongside his old BOQ hotel, waiting for her brother, waiting for Habermann to return to her in his *xich-lo*. He asks everyone on the street, he rambles through alleys, he goes to the Thanh-Bich, but no one remembers her, has ever even heard of her. Her brother seems never to have existed. The MP in the kiosk is new and he doesn't remember her, either. Eventually, as all else fails, he moves in a dream through Saigon, up and down the streets, into the bars, the back alley whore-houses and blowjob houses, the steam baths and massage parlors, the opium dens and drug houses, the AWOL hotels, every corner of corruption and degradation; he finds plenty of eight-year-old girls, but none of them is Ly. He questions his sanity. Have all these months been some bizarre, twisted dream? Or has she simply disappeared, another street urchin swallowed whole by the war?

He spends his last day packing and looking for her. He doesn't give up completely until he's in the hangar, about to board his Freedom Bird. He stands in the middle of the huge, open building with three hundred others—their duffel bags lined up like green caterpillars out of dreams—and he becomes amazed. He shakes his head. He even laughs out loud. Freedom Bird. How could he have expected anything so wonderful out of something so awful?

But as he waits the last few minutes, he tries to imagine what it would be like if this were not a troop ship, if she were here with him. She'd sit in the seat next to him; he'd buckle her in; he'd pat her small hand and give her a candy bar and some gum to chew to keep her ears from popping. And he'd assuage her fears. There's nothing to it, he'd tell her. Soon they'll bring her a Coke, and before she knows it, she'll be asleep and they'll land in America. And her new life, their new lives, will begin. He has so many things to show her. His wife—her mother—will meet their plane and they'll get acquainted while he processes out. She shouldn't worry. She'll love her new mother.

Habermann's formation shoulders duffel bags, heads out into the heat, treks quickly across the concrete and begins up the stairway to the plane to freedom. But before he reaches his first step up, Habermann turns, and from out of nowhere, across the war-ravaged runway, as if out of a sentimental fantasy, a glorious past where impossible things really do come true, she runs toward him, Ly, her small child's arms outstretched to him, her savior, her father.

FIRE

LATE ONE NIGHT, after a particularly horrendous drunken debauch at the enlisted men's club, the day and swing shifts of the Bien-Hoa 125th Electronic Intelligence Company began building a bonfire. They dragged things from out of the barracks, from all over the company, and heaped them up: paper, books, chairs, tables, beds, radios, stereos, records, footlockers, fatigues, underwear, socks, boots, and rifles. Some went out into the surrounding fields for sticks and logs and dry grass. They piled and piled and piled. And then they piled some more.

After two hours, the pile had gotten way up beyond the roofs of the barracks, even up over the tin mess hall, and finally, above the highest building of all, the giant, loudly humming operations building where they did all their secret things, higher and higher, until everyone was naked and there was nothing left, nothing except what was inside the officers' barracks where the officers slumbered.

Later, someone went to the generator shack, filled a can with kerosene, crawled gingerly all the way to the top, and doused it. And while he was up there, he dug around naked as a jaybird until he found two short poles, a sock, and a fatigue shirt. He fashioned a clumsy cross and draped it.

No one knew that the air base even had fire trucks, but in no time they came roaring up the dusty base road, spinning their lights and blaring their sirens. They had the fire out in minutes. Then they moved slowly and silently back down the base road, like moon cars, dragging the blackness behind them.

After the fire was out, all of the enlisted men were forced to stand naked in formation in the company street, behind the looming, pulsating operations building. The officers strutted, postured, hollered, raved, and cursed. They paced in front of their men, berating them, each taking his turn.

One said they were a disgrace to the uniform, that they weren't fit to wear that sacred dress. Another said it was mutiny, revolution of the worst order, insurrection of the most disgusting kind.

But the men paid no mind. They yawned, picked their noses, scratched their behinds, and caressed their genitals. They stood firm and spoke not a word.

Finally, the commander addressed the men. The consequences would be dire, he said, most dire indeed, unless the men were willing to return to the way things had been. They would suffer dearly for this as it was, so they had better get their asses in gear. He may even send them *out there,* out where the end of the world was. They knew where the world ended, didn't they? he asked, smiling maliciously and pointing out toward the perimeter into the unknown creepy night. And he would send them as they were, naked, alone, and weaponless, one at a time. And he could do it. Make no mistake, he could do it.

The men went to work at once. They cleaned up the debris, shoveled, graded, and raked the dust. They were issued new underwear, new fatigues, new boots, and new rifles. After they were dressed, they went to the base PX and bought new stereos, new radios, and new books. When they returned to the company, they unloaded the truckload of new tables, chairs, beds, and footlockers that was waiting there for them and refilled the barracks. By the time midshift finished, all was in place. Everyone nodded and smiled and shook his head. Dayshift went to work and swingshift went to bed. Midshift went to the club.

In no time, the fire slipped far into their long ago memories, until eventually, it almost disappeared all together. They nearly forgot anything had happened, and finally they decided that maybe nothing ever had.

DOING WHAT ROGER SAID

I RIDE BUSES, those that run on and on for hundreds of miles, cramping your legs and frying your brains. I take nothing less than five hundred miles, and I don't get off more than I'm forced to. The fewer changes I have to make the better. Greyhound Americruiser Service and Jefferson the Energy Saver. San Francisco–New York, Minneapolis–Laredo, Los Angeles–Boston, I've ridden them all.

I'm never without my pistol, a snubnosed twenty-five that I keep in the green windbreaker that I never take off for more than a minute. I often slip my hand in my pocket to make sure it's still where it belongs. It keeps me company, and touching it there makes me feel good.

I love buses, but I hate bus terminals. They're always so greasy and seedy and crowded, and I'm afraid. The people press in on me and force me to grip my twenty-five, especially the blacks. They strut around with earrings in their ears and snap their fingers. They stare at me. I've always had trouble with blacks, especially in the army. They kept to themselves, but they seemed like beings from another planet already then. They could just as well have had five eyes and doorknobs in the middle of their heads.

I spend as little time in bus terminals as possible, though sometimes, of course, I have to. I have to buy tickets and food and books and change buses. I have to wash my clothes and I need the exercise too.

I buy all my food from the terminal machines—liverwurst, bologna, summer sausage, and ham and cheese. Ham and cheese is my favorite, though sometimes the cheese is rancid. The fruit usually isn't much good, the apples are soft and the oranges are juiceless and stringy, but I don't like food much anymore, anyway. Sometimes I think I could get along without food.

I learned to be a great reader in the army. There was always so much time to read. I read anything I could get my hands on, but I like science fiction the best, and the terminal racks are always filled with them. *The Intergalactic Wars, The Marriage of Dune,* Isaac Asimov, Robert Heinlein, and Arthur C. Clarke. I buy seven or eight at a stop. When I'm finished with them, I leave them in the brown paper sack they came in, on a terminal waiting room seat for somebody else to find. Sometimes I leave messages in the margins, like "Great Stuff." Or if I'm in the mood, "You'll never know me," or sometimes just "Fuck You."

When I get to a terminal where I have to change, after I've bought my ticket or found my new bus and bought what I need, I force myself to walk from one end of the station to the other until my bus receives its final call. This terrifies me, and I walk in constant fear, but I force myself ruthlessly because I know I need the exercise. The larger the terminal, the better the exercise, and with the really big ones like Chicago, it takes me an excruciatingly long time to go from one end of the terminal to the other. And there are often dark corners where I know awful things must be going on, but I refuse to look. I know the exercise is good for me, but knowing does nothing about the fear I feel.

And sometimes, the worst times of all, are when I have to wash and shave and wash my clothes. I'm usually able to keep myself shaved and clean enough with a thermos of water and the bus toilet, even though diesel fuel has become such a part of me that I'm now no different from those who creep out of the hatches of submarines after days at sea—the smell has not only seeped into my clothes, but into my skin. But every two or three weeks I force myself to shave and wash thoroughly in a terminal restroom. I pick the best times possible for this—three or four o'clock in the morning in a small-town stop. I wait until there's no one else around, and then I quickly strip, shave, wash, and dress again.

But even worse are my clothes. When the time comes, I'm filled with dread beyond belief, but they have to be washed, so I change and head for the nearest laundromat. I keep my eyes trained on the ground as I walk. I've always detested the dirty clothes and bleach stink of laundromats. When there are other people, I wait and stare at the dryer going round and round, fondling my pistol, as the dryer whirls and tumbles and slides. When I'm alone I pace.

I used to be more relaxed and spend more time in bus terminals. I used to like them; I liked the change. But that was before I got robbed. I was in a toilet stall in Cleveland, with my pants still around my ankles, when the stall door kicked in hard against my knees. This black kid about sixteen stood there with a knife. He had one of those big silver and black watches around his wrist, the kind that tell the date and the weather report, and what time it is in Vientiane. He was grinning at me, and I could tell right away that the big kick for him was the toilet part, catching people with their pants down.

"Gimme your money, honkie motherfucker."

He stood there and grinned and his voice didn't quaver. He liked his work fine, I could see that. I never even bothered to pull up my pants. I just slipped the pistol out of my pocket and watched until the restroom door closed behind his back.

So I stay on the bus until it's time for me to force myself out into the terminal again. Every time, my stomach jumps around like I have a frog inside, and I get the runs. Having the runs in a chemical toilet used to bother me, but I got used to that, too.

Vietnam was where I learned about buses, but that was before I shot Roger. Roger was my best friend, the only friend I ever had. When we'd see a bus going down the road while we were on patrol, he'd tap me on the shoulder. "Look at them buses, Jay," he'd say. "Now there's the ticket." They moved down the road slow as turtles, grinding gears, food piled over the top rack, squawking chickens stuffed upside down in crates. Roger would stop me and point with his M-16. "Where you think them buses are going, Jay? It don't matter, does it?" He'd shake his head and laugh. "We gotta keep moving, too, Jay, or we gonna get greased." We'd start stepping along and catch up with the rest of the patrol. "That's what we gotta remember. Think you can remember that for me, Jay?"

When I left Oakland after discharge, there was a bus boarding for New York and I got on. As I watched the countryside fly by, the Plains, the Midwest, and then the East, I thought how wonderful it was that the bus was so warm and toasty and how cold it was outside. It was snowing hard then, everywhere, like it's snowing now, and the earth was frozen black and white wherever I looked, like death. When I'd left Saigon twenty hours before, it was 105 degrees and the water poured down my face as I stood on the gray runway in formation. Vietnamese women squatted in the shade near a fence, fanning themselves with their straw conical hats, quacking away like ducks in their funny language, taking a break from filling sandbags. One had her leg stuck out into the sun, and her black silk pants leg shown like a mirror. I could see the green swampy jungle just off the end of the runway. I clenched my fists and waited for the mortars I knew would begin falling. But even though they never came, I knew right then that Roger had been right.

After I inherited the money it was easy. I have enough now to ride buses for the rest of my life and then some. A great uncle on my dad's side I never knew, never even heard of, left it to me, like the movies, like destiny. It was the last mail I bothered to pick up at the box I rented on a trip through Minneapolis. Who needs mail now? It was just another trip away from the bus.

When I'm not reading, or thinking about Roger, or worrying about the next terminal, sometimes I think about my parents. I haven't seen either of them in fifteen years, but I still think about them from time to time. I wonder if they're dead.

My ma's the toughest person I've ever known. She stands five feet three, weights about eighty-five pounds, and smokes Pall Mall straights down to the tip. She grew up in a family of eight kids on a farm ten miles from where I was raised, in northern Wisconsin, and she had to scrape and claw and gouge for everything she had. She always told me that she could never figure her mother going through labor more than once. When she had me she knew that one goddamn kid was enough for one lifetime. We lived in an old green mobile home on a trailer park near the edge of town. I slept on a rollaway bed in the living room, and both of us couldn't fit in the kitchen at the same time. Paint flaked off the side of the trailer like it had a disease, and you could've run through the walls. My ma worked all day at a dingy shoe factory for piecework wages where people took after each other with scissors over one extra twenty-five-cent piece of work. She never cooked my meals or washed my clothes. She spent every night in D.J.'s bar down the road, just under the rail viaduct, drinking beer and shots of brandy. When I was in the army, she moved and never volunteered her new address.

My dad and I always got along, but he just never got the hang of steady work and family life. I understand that now. He bought me an old, gray '50 Pontiac when I was sixteen to drive back and forth to school. It had fluid drive but it always stuck somehow, and I'd have to wind it up till it nearly busted in every gear, rattling the sides and shaking the fenders. The cloth seats were worn through on the driver's side and smelled like rotting foam rubber. He always bought me little gifts, too, like watches and silver key chains. Last I heard, he was in prison in Georgia for cashing bad checks.

I did well in school, the best in my class. It always came easy for me, but I got into trouble. I stole hubcaps and side mirrors and batteries and fuzzy little dice. And once in a while, a whitewall tire or two. I'd sell them to whoever I could find. I had a good little business going, until I sold to the wrong person and the police staked out the used car lot. They caught me with a bag of side mirrors.

I needed the money. My ma was never home, and if I wanted to buy candy bars or soda, or if I wanted to buy anything for my car, I had to make the money myself. Or even if I wanted to go to the movies. Stealing for the money just seemed like the natural thing to do.

In those days they still gave you a choice of reform school or the army, especially with Vietnam going full tilt. I can still see the judge like I can see this blue, sweat-stained seat in front of me. He wore wire-rimmed glasses and was so short that he barely reached the top of the bench, like he was in a highchair. He seemed so like someone out of Laurel and Hardy or The Three Stooges that I had to keep from laughing.

He did me a favor, though. He gave me three years in the army, and it was the best thing anyone ever did for me. I was upset about it at the time, of course—I couldn't finish high school, I had to leave home, all that—though I've no idea now what I thought I wanted to stay in northern Wisconsin for. But the army straightened me right out; it really did. When I'd complain about extra guard duty or powdered eggs or another patrol to nowhere, Roger'd smile at me like an angel. He really looked like an angel. He had a shock of brown hair that hung over his forehead and the whitest, most perfect teeth I've ever seen. He was tall, too, and big, bigger than anyone in the company by far. He towered over us all like the good giant. He could've been an angel. He really could have.

"If it wasn't for the army, Jay," he'd say, "you wouldn't have met me. Then where would you be?"

He was right, too. I sure miss Roger.

* * *

The bus drivers are all the same. In ten years I haven't run into many new ones. I never talk to them, but often they'll smile or nod or wink at me. I used to memorize their names from the nameplates above their heads—right up there with the smoking regulations and the sign telling everybody to remain behind the white line—but most of them don't even have nameplates anymore.

Each bus has a different howl, and the farther toward the back, toward the engine, the more I can tell each one. People forget, it happens so seldom, but buses break down. I can always tell when something's about to happen. The howl will become a whine, like fifty bees in your ear. It's like somebody's inside trying to get your attention, or like somebody's inside trying to get out.

Sometimes people'll get under my skin. There was this kid once, on a trip from New York to San Francisco. Outside Saint Louis he began singing "Old McDonald Had a Farm." He had a voice like someone was pressing up and down on a record, over and over, up and down. And he repeated the same ten words again and again. He was making the whole bus miserable. I heard his mother tell the woman next to her that they were going all the way to San Francisco, so I turned around in my seat and told her if she didn't muzzle him, I'd stuff him down the chemical toilet. I think everybody on the bus was glad except the kid and his ma. Why she didn't tell him to shut up, I don't know. Maybe she didn't hear him. People are funny about their kids. They don't hear. I've got a lot of time to notice these things.

I never want to talk with other riders, but sometimes I can't help it. Some people'll have it no other way, no matter how surly I look, no matter how many times I turn away without answering. If they only knew what I have in my windbreaker pocket. I go for weeks without saying a word out loud. And when I can't get out of it, the first time I open my mouth, my voice croaks and cracks like my ma's used to in the morning before work.

A few years ago, on a bus from Minneapolis to Laredo, I met a fourteen-year-old kid who was really taken with me. I don't know why. I wouldn't be taken with me. But who knows? She probably thought I was wonderful because I was so different from her ma and pa and all her little fourteen-year-old boyfriends. Why she was traveling alone at that age on a mangy night bus, I don't know. Before she got off in Mason City, Iowa, she rubbed my leg and pecked my cheek and invited me to call her up, to stop and see her the next time I passed through Mason City. I looked down at her soft tender face—she was a gorgeous little thing, all smooth skin and creamy blonde—and wondered where she learned all that stuff at her age. I said, sure, right, maybe I will at that. But there's no way I'll ever leave the buses.

I like it best when the bus isn't crowded and I get two seats to myself. Then I can spread out and read or sleep or do what I want. But best of all, I like the ones with only a couple of people on the whole bus. That used to happen a lot on night trips in the winter.

I remember one time. We were riding through upstate New York on the Thruway, between Buffalo and Rochester. It was snowing like crazy then, too. I was new. It was only my third trip. It had snowed for days, twenty to twenty-five inches, and drifted huge mounds all over the highway. I'll never know why they didn't close the Thruway. We were breaking through drift after drift, and sometimes we'd stop and push a car along the way, the three of us, the other rider, the bus driver, and me. The bus driver'd holler back, "You guys ready for another one?" and we'd pile out into the snow. I don't even remember what the driver and the other rider looked like, but the snow impressed me so. We'd pound out into the snow and push, and it was like a moon-scape out there, like we were all alone in the universe. When I looked around into the night on the deserted Thruway, the snow blowing hard into my face, I forgot where I was. Where am I? I wondered.

Later, as we neared Rochester, there were no more cars to push, and we rode through the night alone. The other rider and I switched on the overhead lights, and then we could no longer see the snow, but we knew it was there, pelting the bus and icing the windshield. The driver battled on, and we were like a beacon, inching along the highway in the night, the last speck of humanity in a world gone empty and barren of life.

I knew then that I'd never get off. I could see so clearly all the years ahead of me. I could see myself as I am now, sitting here in this blue-checkered bus seat, watching the snow falling in the night, until I shrivel and die like a crusty grasshopper, swept into the corner of the bus to rot and disappear.

* * *

But today, on this bus bound for nowhere in particular, I'm having one of my days. The snow is getting worse, and I feel lonely, something I'm feeling more and more these days. It's a change that frightens me. I forget where we're headed, what bus I'm on. What difference does it make anyway, I think, whether it's Boston or Chicago or Los Angeles or Kai Kai, Nebraska?

But even more disturbing to me is that I'm beginning to remember more and more vividly the smell of bacon frying and the feel of a soft bed—I haven't slept in a bed for ten years—and I remember coffee brewing and baseball games and following the pennant race and the World Series. And I think how it could've been—sometimes I even have dreams like it really happened. And I think again about trying to get off, about stealing myself and getting off for good, but I know I never will. I think of Roger, and then I remember that I killed him.

* * *

Sometimes I get confused. It seems now that the snow was falling then, too, like it is now, piling again along the roadway, freezing and icing the world. But I know it couldn't have been. It must've been hot like it always was, the sun at you and at you without end, until even your eyelids burned—the green jungle leaves brown with dust, swaying and dancing to the pop, pop, popping helicopter blades like music.

But there was no music.

"No, no, Jay, listen, it's all right. I know you didn't mean it. It's all right." He smiled. He slapped my hand hard, like I'd just hit a home run. "I shoulda kept moving, Jay."

Listen: He said it was all right.

It's all right, Jay, he said.

So I'm doing what he said. I promised him; I promised Roger. I'll do it, Roger, I said. Let the snow fall and the buses roll, I'll always do what Roger said. See, Roger, I'm doing it. Watch me now, Roger. I haven't forgotten. I'll never forget. You can count on me. See? See, Roger?

VOLLEYBALL

EARLY ONE MORNING, at a joint Vietnamese/American camp deep in the Ia-Drang Valley, Special Forces and ARVN Rangers began playing volleyball. They strung a ragged net from two tall trees and played furiously, like men driven by forces unknown and incomprehensible. They played as the score mounted, as the ball slammed back and forth, all morning and all afternoon long.

And when they could no longer see the ball, and it began bouncing off heads and tipping off blind fingers, to be searched for in the high grass and tall weeds, they drove all their jeeps, deuce-and-a-halves, APCs, half tracks, and tanks onto the course. When the lights were turned on, the place lit up like the sun had dropped into the jungle.

Then they went back at it once again. They played to a hundred points, to two hundred and more. They showed no signs of fatigue, their eyes clear and flashing, wet with concentration, their legs solid as trees. It seemed they would play on forever.

But as morning neared, they started showing evidence of tiring. Their arms began to weaken, their legs wobbled, and their eyes clouded over with wandering thoughts. Sweat caused them to remove their fatigue pants and play in their green GI boxer shorts. They began to miss easy shots and to trip and to fall. They began thinking of other things.

Finally, as dawn crept out and above the trees, they stopped completely. They stopped all at once, without words, without any real warning. They dropped their hands to their sides, stared briefly at one another across the net, and walked off the court. They put on their uniforms, strapped on their gear, saddled up, and moved out into the morning jungle.

After the match, they went about their work with a new zest and sense of adventure. And a camaraderie entered things. They could depend on each other for the first time. They regained interest in the war, and fun came back into their lives.

SWANN

AFTER ALL THESE years, those early morning talks on the sand-rise still play over and over like a film locked forever inside my head, the projector clicking in the dark, the dust particles flying against the glare, the three of us, Swann, Chavez, and me, grinning out of this white wall in front of me. And the main attraction has been the morning Swann told us he'd volunteered airborne.

It was a Sunday, the last night before graduation from basic training at Fort Leonard Wood. Our bags were packed, our weapons cleaned and inspected, and our uniforms pressed and laid out on our bunks in preparation for the morning march to graduation. It was our last night together, and so much was in the past by then, the interminable drills, the bayonets, the ceaseless harassment. We'd begun to relax. We'd even smuggled along two six-packs of beer.

We needed our sleep, but in those days, we needed the talk more. It was June of '66, and more than fifty thousand had been drafted in our month alone. Vietnam was on our minds all the time. It seemed there was nothing else then.

And it was such a mystery to us. Suddenly we were in basic training. I was carrying out groceries one day and lugging an M-16 the next. Leonard Wood was filled with whole battalions of air-headed zombies shuffling about in the sand. As companies marched past on the streets, the men stared at each other, as if to say, What the fuck is this and why has it come about just in time for us?

Most of our talk that morning, Chavez's and mine, was about going home that next day. Some of us had bought plane tickets; for me it would be my first time on an airplane. Chavez had joined with some others to charter a bus. But Swann was from Saint Louis, and he wasn't interested in plane tickets or chartered buses. He had other things on his mind.

The sandrise was a barren lump of waste, not far from the post movie theatre. From the third week on we sneaked out of bed and sat up there with our cigarettes and talked half the night. A peaceful dark settled over the whole post by the time we got there at two o'clock—the only sound distant, occasional cries of disgust from company mess hall cooks and KPs preparing for the morning eruption. Near dawn the frying fat and egg stink forced us back down to our barracks.

Up on the rise those mornings we talked about what was going to happen next and what we could do about it. We should go to Waynesville and catch venereal disease on the strip, Swann suggested. He'd heard about one guy who showed up for sick call every single morning for a month, with something new each time. Finally, they got sick of him and let him out. Chavez'd heard about somebody who got out for flat feet. And everyone had heard of the psycho cases. We even had one in our company. He woke up one morning mumbling and headed for the razor blades. They discharged him unfit for military service. And who wasn't unfit? I'm unfit, Chavez said, I'm unfit as fuck. We were all unfit.

Or Chavez and Swann talked about where they were going after they went AWOL. Swann was going to Vancouver and open a jazzy soul food joint with live entertainment. Chavez was heading for Quebec, so he could sell deepfried catfish to all those French Canadian girls. And me. I had a plan, too, but I didn't need to go AWOL.

Once I'd received my draft notice, I was shocked to realize that I could still enlist. Not only that, but the army would guarantee that I'd be sent to language school. All I had to do was sign on for four years. So I'd enlisted to keep out of the war, and I had everything planned perfectly. I'd be sent to study Japanese or Russian or Outer Mongolian, maybe. I envisioned a sort of combination health spa language school, where I wandered about through steam rooms of towel-clutching women, speaking in tongues, 15,000 miles from the war.

Swann and Chavez made fun of me, of course. They were draftees and each had decided to take his chances. Two years of the army was all anyone should have to take, Chavez said. It was all anyone could stomach. And why trust the army? Swann rolled his eyes. They got something in mind, sure, for a dumb mother-fucker like you. They both laughed at me, and I felt I deserved it, hoping with all my heart that they weren't right.

* * *

Chavez lit a Pall Mall and flipped his Zippo to Swann. The lighter flashed on Swann's face and quickly snapped closed again. Chavez popped a beer can.

"Fuck, boys," said Chavez. He placed his hands behind his head and leaned backward and forward, like he was rocking a chair. He looked like a man who just discovered he had all of creation spread out before him.

"This shit, man, fuck. No time at all now, they seen their last of Chavez."

Chavez was huge—rough and knotty, like an elm tree. I touched his forearm once, and it felt like pliable metal. His big, gap-toothed grin made him look like a hillbilly from the movies. When I first met him, he reminded me of somebody right off, but I couldn't place who it was. I forgot about it until it came to me months later in the middle of the night. Andy Griffith in *No Time for Sergeants*. Chavez was from Missouri, too, Joplin. I didn't think about all of this Missouri business then, but I had other things on my mind in those days.

Chavez grinned and looked at his wristwatch. He slapped me on the leg.

"That pussy'll be linin' up about this time, all the way down Murray Street, just waitin' for good old Chavez."

"Shit, man," said Swann, pointing his Kool like a high school teacher at a blackboard. "That pussy ain't waitin' for no dumb fuckin' dickhead like you."

I laughed and reached for one of the six packs. I was all jazzed up that morning, high on the truth of my fantasies and delusions. When I tried to light a cigarette, I dropped it into the sand twice before I got it lit. Then I lit the wrong end. I got language school orders just like I had it planned. They were for Vietnamese, of course, but what the hell? I had it all figured already. The war would be over by the time my language class finished in a year. And even if it wasn't, I'd be too valuable by then to be sent into the war. I'd monitor Vietnamese transmissions from Okinawa or Japan or maybe from Timbuktu. Or from a ship six hundred miles off the coast. I'd be set for sure, I told myself. I told myself a lot of things then.

"Fuck, boy," Chavez grinned and slapped me on the leg again. He pointed to the burning filter. "Didn't nobody teach you to smoke in Minnesota? Or all them people up there got frozen brains?"

I shoved the filter into the sand. Chavez'd gotten artillery, so he was all right, too. He'd heard all about it from a DI that morning—safe, triple-row sandbag bunkers, eight inch guns, basecamps and rear areas.

I looked at Swann. His cigarette lay on his lower lip, his beer can propped on his knee. His T-shirt was so white against his black skin that it seemed to glow in the dark. He was going to be a clerk, and I thought then how natural that was. He was just the type, the one who took care of things. That kind of stuff gets around fast—who you can trust, and who you can't, who gets things done, and who doesn't. And they all came to Swann, even the DIs. When they needed a runner or a message delivered, they headed for Swann.

I was thinking how we'd all three made it after all, how we'd all made out just fine and how pleased I was, when Chavez broke into song. He got up and danced around like a madman, a regular Al Jolson.

"Swannie, how I love ya, how I love ya, my dear old Swannie. . . ."

Swann threw his beer as hard as he could, splashing it against Chavez's T-shirt. Chavez stopped and laughed like a giant in the night, his hands on his hips. But Swann didn't laugh back. He just mumbled and looked at the ground. He reached for another beer, but after he opened it, he set it in the sand. I felt soda water bubble through my balls.

Swann threw his cigarette down in front of him.

"I ain't gonna be no clerk."

Chavez sat down, and I got up on one knee, like I was about to take off. Swann shoved his hands into the sand at his sides.

"I volunteered airborne today."

He tried to laugh but failed and closed his mouth. He kept his hands in the sand, his arms tightening, like he was balancing himself. His face shone silvery black in the moonlight. I looked at Chavez. His eyes flickered, like they were wet.

"I got a little brother," he said, as if that explained everything. I tried to see his eyes, but he'd turned away from us. "He's seventeen and he's the only one I got left. I promised the old man."

He stood and kicked the beer can over into the sand.

"Nam. Airborne'll get me there sure."

We knew there was no use asking—talking and pleading would come to nothing. He was looking out beyond us, toward one of the mess hall lights. He'd finished and shut up about it for good. We knew he was asking for it, and I knew damn well what he meant, though I had to put all the pieces together myself later. I looked at Chavez again, and he shook his head slowly. He had the saddest expression I'd ever seen, and it shocked me to see him like that. But it was a terrible thing, someone committing suicide before your eyes.

* * *

I grew up on a pig farm in southern Minnesota, ten miles from the Iowa border, and Swann was the first black man I'd ever known. Before basic training, the only blacks I'd ever seen were on TV, like Rochester on "The Jack Benny Show." I'd never been more than fifty miles from the farm, and when I first arrived at Fort Leonard Wood, I was terrified and appalled by babyshit-colored buildings filled with jiving, handslapping blacks from the streets of Chicago and Gary, Indiana.

I kept to myself in the reception center, trying to slide about unseen, fading out as much as possible, fading back in only when I had to. I tried not to faint in the shot line so I wouldn't be singled out for humiliation and ridicule by one of the swagger-stick-swinging DIs. And I made sure I remembered to shave each morning, too, even though a ten-year-old girl has more beard than I had then. I wasn't taking any chances of being dry shaved in front of the whole company by a sadistic DI. I kept my mouth shut unless someone asked me something, until I pulled guard duty the fourth night.

Guard duty consisted of sitting up all night in the barracks while others slept, keeping an eye out for fires and sudden musters by drunken DIs. There weren't enough days in the reception center for everyone to draw guard, but I drew it and so did Swann.

We talked about everything that night, like basic trainees do, and by morning we were old friends. Knowing that there is nowhere to go and nothing you can do about it makes you talk. And pride had already gone with the haircut.

He told me about his family, and I told him about mine. He was from East Saint Louis—him, his older sister, and his little brother. There had been three other brothers, too, but they were all dead by that time, killed in the streets in one way or another. His mother and father were long separated and long dead, his father from a knife wound in his ribs over a cheap bottle of wine in an East Saint Louis alley, and his mother from a push out an eighth floor apartment window by a jealous lover. So Swann had taken care of his sister and his little brother. He'd done it since he was fifteen. He'd promised the old man long before he took that knife over cheap booze. Swann knew he was crazy to, but he took promises to heart, even those made to no good motherfuckers like his old man.

I couldn't get enough of his stories, black stories, the tough, abandoned ghetto life he'd lived. How had he even stayed alive, I wondered? It was all so horrible to me, and so fascinating, me a pig farmer's son from southern Minnesota where all I had to worry about was whether or not I made the team. But it was all so natural to Swann. He'd smile gently at me, smoking slowly, pulling on his cigarette, savoring every drag. Hadn't everyone's father been knifed? Wasn't everyone's mother more concerned about a lover than her family? Didn't everyone carry a gun, or at least a knife, to school?

And I was amazed at first by his skin. I couldn't get enough of that, either. I always wanted to touch him, to feel his blackness. I grabbed his arm or patted him on the back just for an excuse to feel him. And he must have known; he looked at me funny sometimes and rolled his eyes. Then he laughed and teased me about something else.

And I often thought, Jesus, here I am and my best friend is black as the ace of spades. Isn't that something? I tried to imagine how my high school friends would react. I was smug about it, of course, as smug as any nineteen-year-old. Wow, I had a black friend. But it wasn't long before all that wore off; I knew that he was the best friend I ever had, and I forgot about the rest.

I listened to everything he said; I tried to catch every word. He was so wise. Why he took to me I'll never know. What did he want with a pig farmer's son? I didn't know then, and I don't know now, though I've thought about it plenty since then. I'd like to ask him. And there's a lot of other stuff I'd like to ask him, too, like why he had to do it, why he couldn't forget about promises made to dead winos.

After that night, we were talking all the time. I'll admit I hovered over him. He was my protection at first, until I got used to things as they were. I used him like a shield.

Once we got to our basic training unit, Chavez slept below Swann, and I slept in the next upper. We all took to each other, and soon we were inseparable. Later, we began heading for the sandrise at two o'clock.

So I knew what Swann's volunteering airborne was all about, and I'm sure Chavez knew, too. Swann needed to go to Vietnam in order to take care of his brother and sister. He'd get about sixty extra dollars a month for his sister by volunteering airborne, and as long as he remained in Vietnam, his little brother wouldn't have to go. And if Swann got killed, his brother would be a last surviving son, and he wouldn't have to go then, either. All Swann had to do was stay in Vietnam until the war was over, or until he got killed, whichever came first.

* * *

Then I saw Swann over there. It hadn't turned out badly for me. I was on a basecamp in IV Corps and only had to worry about mortars and rockets. We ran twelve hour shifts in a radio truck, searching frequencies for the voice communications that the VC never used. Twelve on, twelve off. The year passed fast enough. And I'd seen Chavez, too, but things hadn't turned out so good for him.

He was on a firebase ten klits west of us, and one Sunday afternoon we made a run over there to see their commander. Three of their 155s had dropped short and landed near some of our antennas. I hadn't walked fifty feet from the truck that afternoon when I saw him. They'd been nearly overrun by a ground attack the month before, and they had to swing their 155s straight down, firing point blank into the perimeter at the oncoming VC. They'd made it, but there are lots of ways of making it, and I wasn't prepared for what I saw.

Before the ground attack I could imagine what it had been like, laughing and enjoying the safety of those sandbag bunkers, firing rounds out into the jungle on people he never saw. He could have been working 155s in Joplin, for all he knew. But now he'd lost that Andy Griffith grin. He looked frightened and hopped up, his eyes grown wide, his body shrunken and small next to the split sandbags and the jutting black tubes. He had on earflaps like stereo headphones. He reminded me of a retarded kid back home, a huge hearing aid strapped over his ears. I waited for the first bang and watched Chavez twitch a second before the crack of the gun. I watched them fire a few more rounds, then I turned away and walked back to the truck.

Swann came to my basecamp one morning with a supply truck. I'd been in country eight months by that time, and I never expected to see him again. But I saw him when the truck rolled in, high up on the sides of the box. He didn't get off the truck with the others. He sat there the whole hour they were in camp, just sitting up there and not moving. I stood right down below the box and called his name once or twice, but he never moved. He was full of red dust, even his lips had dust on them. As I looked up at him, I tried to remember him in a white T-shirt, rolling his eyes and smiling at something naive I had said, a Kool in his lips, on the sandrise at Fort Leonard Wood.

I stood there for half an hour. There was no breeze, and I swear not even his eyelashes moved. Then they all piled back on, and I watched the truck head off, kicking red dust as it roared out into the jungle toward the rim of the world, him up on the rack, his hands in his lap, staring, like a black Buddha.

I knew his sister's address in East Saint Louis; we'd exchanged before we left basic training, but I never bothered to call on her when I got back. I knew he was dead. I never called on Chavez, either. He didn't need to hear from me.

But Swann. I hope his kid brother appreciates it. I know it isn't fair to hate him. He's probably good, maybe even a little like Swann. If I try hard, I can sometimes see him as a younger edition, a hint of that soft, gentle smile, a Kool hanging on his lower lip. Maybe he even rolls his eyes the way his brother used to. I know it isn't fair to hate him, but it isn't fair that Swann should be dead, either.

And so the reel plays on, and I am taught to forget, that all I need to do is forget. And sometimes I even try. But the reel plays on, and there's nothing I can do to stop it, nothing I can do at all. Yet part of me is content, because I know that as long as the reel continues, the three of us—Swann, Chavez, and me—are still young and forever alive on this white wall in front of me.

DOING SHAKESPEARE

THE MORNING MEYER returned home, a week after he'd crept out of the jungles, leaving his fellow LURPs behind, his .45 pistol and his skinning knife still tucked into his belt, he bought an orange Volkswagen with a black stripe down the middle. He and his father stood in the used car lot, the wind whipping snow into circles and spraying it over the hoods of the cars into their faces. They had tassel caps down over their ears, their shoulders hunched against the cold. The salesman hadn't even bothered to come outside, but had stayed in his heated shack a hundred feet away. Meyer's father shook his head and kicked a tire. His moustache had streaked with gray in the last three years, and he'd developed a belly that pushed his brown corduroy coat out in front of him like he was concealing a basketball. He looked down at the ground and scraped the snow with his boot. Don't make a mistake, he said—the brakes were spongy and the clutch slipped. And the color: My God, it was a joke. He kicked another tire. Don't do it, he said.

Meyer arrived unannounced earlier that morning after riding a day and a half on a Greyhound bus from San Francisco. His mother and father had bought a new house while he'd been gone, and he'd stood in the middle of the tiny living room, his duffel bag still at his feet, listening to his mother as she told him vacantly that she was sorry, but, as he could see, they really had no room for him in their new little house, that for the time being he'd have to sleep on a folding cot in the kitchen and keep his shaving cream and safety razor in the cupboard with the dishes. She'd been about to go to the hairdresser's and had worn a green and white gingham dress and a patent leather handbag across her arm. On her way out the door, she'd pecked him on the cheek and patted his hand.

* * *

Meyer headed out of northern Wisconsin toward Interstate 90 and Madison beyond. He had some old friends to visit, friends he hadn't seen since high school. As he worked through the gears, watching the dark green, snow-covered pine forests slip by both sides of the highway and wait for him at the end of his vision, he remembered how in high school they would sit most every night in his father's '50 Chevrolet on the street in front of the old Lutheran church, four overweight, bespectacled adolescents, sipping illegal beer, sharing their versions of the future, dreaming of women and power. In their senior year they had even played Shakespeare—*A Midsummer's Night's Dream*—the four of them leads, transformed into agile, deep-throated young men, leaping about the hushed stage in the eerie twilight. The audience— nearly the whole town—packed into the eighty degree heat of the small gymnasium had stood and applauded wildly, for hours it had seemed to them on stage, transported into something beyond itself, the clapping going on and on, their one great moment of high school triumph.

The pine forests were beginning to lighten to birch and poplar, even giving way to a small open field here and there. Noticing that he was still whining along in third gear, Meyer pulled the gearshift back into fourth and pushed his foot to the floor.

* * *

He climbed the stairs to Lauter's apartment and knocked on the door. He thought he heard a voice inside, so he knocked again and pushed the door open. Lauter had a water glass to the wall with his ear pressed to it. He had on a black stocking cap with a red and gold Mao pin attached to the front. Meyer opened his mouth, but before he could greet him, Lauter motioned him over and made him listen, too, made him put his ear up against the glass. Meyer couldn't hear anything, but Lauter could. He could hear the cries and moans of a Chinese couple making love next door.

When Meyer got up close, he noticed that Lauter's sideburns were taped to the sides of his head with scotch tape. Meyer was about to ask him what it was all about when Lauter tapped the sides of his head. It was a preventive measure, he said. He never took his stocking cap off, and he retaped his sideburns every night before bed and every morning after he got up. He was afraid of losing his hair, he said.

Lauter made Meyer sit there with him until noon and watch for the Chinese couple to leave for their one o'clock class. Lauter kept putting his ear to the glass and winking. He had a roommate, he said, who demonstrated against the war. That's where he got the Mao pin. He grinned and gave it a tap. His roommate, he said, talked on and on about the war. He was a real pain in the ass about it. They were always calling rallies and demonstrations, dressing up in old fatigues and green army overcoats.

Lauter lit a cigarette and pushed his stocking cap back a bit on his forehead. He'd lost his baby fat and had a few day's growth of blond beard and a long, uneven, blond moustache. He drank from a warm can of Budweiser, the last of a six-pack, the empty cans scattered about on the floor. He put his feet up on an overturned, cable-spool footrest.

Meyer wanted to ask Lauter if he remembered all those people clapping, if Lauter remembered like he did, or if it had been so long ago that it hadn't really happened the way Meyer remembered. But Lauter continued before Meyer had a chance.

Remember how he, Lauter, used to be into psychology, how he read all those books in high school. Rollo May, Abraham Maslow, Jung. Jesus Christ, spouting all that crap all the time.

Lauter drank more beer and chewed on his wet moustache, maintaining his gaze out the window.

Their teachers thought he was nuts, but they'd been afraid to discourage him. But here, at Madison, Jesus, the shit they'd studied, the shit they'd cared about, expected *him* to care about. It made him sick to see them put all that money into such bullshit, like observing how moles fuck.

Lauter stubbed his cigarette in a jar lid on the cable-spool table and took another swallow. He put the glass to the wall, shook his head, and dropped the glass onto the floor next to him.

Well, he didn't give a fuck about any of it, anymore, and he didn't go to school anymore, either. He hoped his roommate and his cronies took over the world. Those dumb fuckers, could you imagine? Jesus, he grinned and shook his head. Good, he said, he hoped they burned the whole fucking world down. The world deserved it.

Finally, after they saw the Chinese couple strolling hand in hand down the street toward the bus stop, Lauter tossed his last beer can onto the floor, got up, and headed out the door and down the hall toward the toilet. After he left, Meyer lit a cigarette and sat for a few minutes staring at the water glass on the floor and then at an empty book of matches on the windowsill. The matchbook cover advertised bliss through the simple acquisition of an engineering degree in six short weeks at La Salle University. After taking one last look around the room, he headed down the stairs toward his Volkswagen.

* * *

Don was glad to see him. He shook Meyer's hand and hugged him. He slapped him on the back and called him man. Don had lost all his pimples and his baby fat, too, and had grown his brown hair long into a ponytail clasped in the back with a wooden, Indian-looking pin of some kind.

Don was living in a one-room apartment with a woman named Sarah and her three-year-old child, Dayglow. He introduced Sarah to Meyer, but she looked at him without saying a word. She had vacant harassed eyes and long, straight, blonde hair. She sat in a chair and twisted her fingers into a church steeple, opening them up over and over to see all the people. Dayglow sat on her mother's lap and beat a sauce pan off the edge of the chair. She wore a dirty T-shirt with "Heathen Baby" spray-painted across the front.

The walls were bright green, the ceiling a huge yellow sun with purple and red rays shooting from it. A poster next to Meyer's head told him that it was a hot town with pigs in the streets, but that the streets belonged to the people. It asked him if he could dig it.

Sarah's old man was rich, Don said, richer than God himself, even, and they lived off him. He sent a check every month for her and Dayglow. He thought Sarah was still going to school. Don smiled when he said it. They were proud of what they were doing. The old man deserved to be taken advantage of, the capitalist pig bastard, he said.

Don got Meyer a beer and some chartreuse-colored vegetable juice for himself. Beer made him sick now, he said, since he discovered it was just another capitalist plot in the larger scheme to keep the proletariat down. But he still kept some around for his old, unenlightened, capitalist friends, he said, grinning and shaking his ponytail to one side.

Meyer decided to change the subject—he wanted to ask Don about Shakespeare, too—but Don beat him to it. They were demonstrating tomorrow afternoon at the library mall. It was going to be a bad one, he could always tell. There was something in the air. Don actually looked above his head and sniffed. The fucking war. Their plans were a strike in April, when it got warmer. Close the university down. They'd show the fuckers, he said, suddenly pounding his fist hard on the chair, upending the glass and the rest of his vegetable juice onto the floor.

Meyer noticed another poster, on the wall behind Don's head, for the first time. He wanted to ask Don about it, what it meant, why it was on his wall, whether maybe it had anything to do with high school. The poster showed Lyndon Johnson in a long black cape and a peaked black hat. Ding dong, it proclaimed, the wicked witch is dead. Which old witch? The wicked old witch. Ding dong, the wicked witch is dead.

But the war was all Don cared about now. He didn't even *remember* high school anymore, he said. What he must have been like in high school. A fat, pimpled nerd. What was it he was going to do? Law. Fucking *law!* How decadent could you get?

Don laughed and kicked his vegetable juice glass over against the wall. Dayglow's eyes widened and she began to wail, but Sarah, lost in her steeples, said nothing. Don began to shout.

History. Political Science. He knew plenty of both and he hadn't learned them in school, either. He'd learned them where they really counted, with the people, on the streets.

Later, Don and Sarah drifted off into another world, got down on their hands and knees, and spent the rest of the afternoon amusing themselves trying to teach Dayglow to say cocksucker and pass the fucking butter.

* * *

That evening Meyer ran into David drinking beer alone in the University Union Stiftskeller. The dark brown walls were lined with beer steins and elaborate paintings of mock battle scenes with German captions. The room was empty except for David, and in another corner, a group of students gathered about a bearded man in saffron robes.

David hadn't changed. He was still short and fat, his hair was still curly and frizzy, and his glasses still as thick as ever—still the nerd of the world. After Meyer got his beer and sat down, David told him about the man who was trying to kill him.

Every night the man got drunk and forced his way into David's twelfth floor apartment and threatened to throw him out of the window. He ranted and raved and slapped David around, telling him the time wasn't quite right for him to get away with murder yet, but one of these nights, very soon now, zip, boom, out the window he'd go.

The man always had peanut butter in his beard, David said, and his teeth were broken on one side of his mouth. He was so hideous he looked like the Creature from the Black Lagoon. And he'd done it every single night for three months. David was at the end of his rope. He was scared shitless, he said.

David said he talked to the police, but they told him they'd only do something once his head hit the sidewalk out front. They laughed at him, he said. And he hadn't done anything: he'd never even *seen* the man before that first night when he forced his way into his apartment. The injustice, he cried aloud, tears in his eyes. Then, suddenly, he began begging Meyer to protect him. Stay and protect me, Meyer, he said.

The students and the bearded man were filing out. As he headed toward the door, the man's saffron robes billowed wildly, like a wind had come up.

Meyer lit a cigarette and finally asked David if he'd written his novel yet. Maybe David would remember Shakespeare in time, too. Yes, he thought, David was sure to be the one to remember. But David looked at him like he'd lost his mind until Meyer got up and told him as he moved away that he'd write about all this someday, too.

But David just continued staring at him like he'd lost his mind until Meyer cleared the doorway and was out of his vision, headed out past the bar toward the front door and his orange Volkswagen with the black stripe down the center.

* * *

As Meyer left the city it began getting darker and darker. He removed a bottle of whiskey and a .45 pistol from the glove compartment and placed them on the seat. He held the wheel with one hand, uncapped the bottle, and drank from it with the other. After taking another long drink, he wedged the bottle upright between his seat and the middle hump.

He would return to Asia. He had a LURP friend who worked for RMK Construction now, running supplies up the Mekong River. His friend could always use another gunner. Nothing ever changed in Asia.

He looked out at the sky through the windshield and then out into the passing forests and open fields. In the moonlight he saw humpbacked shadows painted with soot sliding down trees, their rifles poking from their packs. He switched on his lights and kept his speed steady, steady toward the west, watching for flares, listening for the flapping of helicopter blades.

He picked up the .45, cocked it, and lay it back on the seat, continuing on through the ever darkening night, through the humpbacked shadows with their rifles, toward the western horizon and the sea beyond that opened before him like a mouth.

* * *

An hour later he entered a small town, pulled off to the side of the road and parked. He grabbed his bottle and his pistol and headed out into the night. As he walked down the street under a leaden sky, he smelled woodpulp from a wood products plant a half mile to the north, its lights blazing against the sky.

A half hour later he found himself in front of an old, red-brick high school. The domed top shown under the reflected light of street lamps like a huge, bald-headed ghost. It appeared ready for the wrecking ball, the windows broken out and the walls painted with scrawled obscenities, like an abandoned warehouse. He imagined rats squeaking merrily across gray-spotted cement floors and peeking out of yellow-trimmed windows. Meyer's own high school was gone now, too. It had had a dome like this one, housing a telescope that had never been used. It had been something about the design.

A car careened around the corner, began to spin and swerve toward Meyer, blaring its horn. He dove into a snowdrift, rolled, and aimed his pistol, but the car eventually righted itself and continued on down the street, roaring and shifting gears.

As Meyer lay in the drift, it began snowing huge, heavy flakes. He turned over on his back, feeling the snow hard and warm along his body. He lay his bare head back into the snow and drank gulps from his bottle, sighting his pistol at tree limbs and second-story windows. He stuck the bottle into the snowbank and spread his arms, making angels in the snow.

Soon the snow began dropping heavier on his lips and cheeks. He got up and walked on. He stumbled and bumped into a tree. He looked up at the snow.

As he trudged back toward where he thought his Volkswagen must be, the snow began falling even more heavily. It came heavier and heavier until he was in danger of losing his way. He pushed ahead but the snow fell on and on, even heavier, and the wind began to blow. He no longer had any idea where his car was, as he put his shoulder to the wind, clutching his .45 to his chest. Finally, later, as he fell toward the street, he heard the sharp joyous cries of fairies spreading their magic spells, and the anguished groans of romantics dying in the snow.

CHRISTMAS HOLIDAY

TWO DAYS BEFORE Christmas the three of us pooled our money and drove to Vancouver in a borrowed '65 Saab without a heater. We drove day and night, wrapped in quilts and thermal underwear, stripping frost with a spatula. At four-thirty in the morning we stopped at a roadside diner outside Medicine Hat. The cook called out from the kitchen that it was twenty-five below zero and that the wind had been clocked at forty miles per hour in gusts. The waitress stood behind the counter with eyes as vacant as snowballs, while we all huddled around a corner table with coffee. We still had our quilts around us. The coffee was tire black and scalding, and I could have poured it over my face. There were hatchets and blankets and six shooters on the walls and a guy in the corner who looked like Orson Welles. The windows rattled when the wind blew hard off the prairie, and finally, after an hour of calling out weather information like food orders, the cook came out from the back room and told us we had to order something besides coffee or leave.

We'd crossed at Emerson Junction at three o'clock in the morning the day before. The customs agent just looked into the car at our beards and waved us on. He wore a gray air force parka with the hood pulled all the way down, so we never even saw his face. As we pulled away, I looked at him out the rear window, moving back toward the door of his shack like a great insect.

94

When we got to Vancouver, we found a hotel for four dollars apiece. A shaggy blond teenager hawked heroin on the third-floor landing, and the guy in the room next door cried all night long because he was alone and broke on Christmas Eve. We watched the Pope on the fading twelve-inch television and smoked cigarettes until dawn. At eight-thirty we went out looking for Willie.

Willie was living in a house on the Bay with a gray and a brown cat. The gray cat was from California and the brown was from Canada. The California cat had only recently been castrated, and he constantly attacked the Canadian cat, which had been neutered for years. He'd jump off the balcony or sneak out from behind the stairs. The fur would fly all day long. The cats would get letters in the mail, and Willie would get down on his hands and knees and read to them.

Willie was housesitting for a doctor and his wife he'd met at a movie. They were leaving the next day for Michigan, they'd said, and they still hadn't found anyone to take care of their house. But they were leaving at 6:00 A.M. anyway, whether they found anyone or not. They didn't care if anyone took care of the house anymore. So Willie said he'd do it, and here he was, with two cats, a freezer full of food, and three refrigerators with all the wire shelves removed and stacked with Molson Ale.

We hadn't seen Willie for thirteen years, since he'd pulled out for Canada. He'd grown a gigantic beard and lost all his hair on top. He worked as a carpenter off and on, and he wore baggy bib overalls with a tape measure in the side pocket all the while we were there. He said over and over that they were still planning to come and get him someday, like Christ. He said he did his best to keep from falling off houses on his worst days.

Willie liked dope now. The rest of us could take it or leave it, but we smoked with him because he said he liked it better that way. So we lined up on the davenport, smoked dope, and drank beer for seven days, watching the ocean waves out the big bay window.

One afternoon Tom stood and began speaking Arabic. He became expansive as he babbled away and strutted around the living room in his old fatigue shirt and baggy, wool pants. Later he started writing Chinese characters on the white kitchen walls with a magic marker. He still had his gray, army-issue glasses held together on one side with a safety pin. His long, curly hair bobbed as he wrote. In the early days he had studied languages at the university. He would study one for a year or so, and then he would travel for six months in the country where they spoke the language he had studied. He had always had a talent for languages. Even in high school he had astounded our teachers by speaking German fluently after only one year. But he hasn't been anywhere lately, not for the last few years. And he hasn't studied anything either. He told me everywhere looks the same after awhile. He'd rather drink beer now. The war ruined us all, he said.

Mauer said he thought it was just the times. We should have been born in the 1920s. Then we'd be all right. Mauer was always saying that. Paris of the twenties. He had a cigarette along the side of his ear like a pencil and one lit in his hand. His dark, hollow face had always fascinated the women we used to know. The two burn holes in his white sweater had increased to three since we had arrived at Willie's. Mauer tried to be a writer, but he failed over and over again. He even stopped taking baths for three months after he read James Joyce. But publishers kept sending everything he wrote back to him, sometimes without even bothering about rejection slips. He wrote poems about lost souls ruined by the war or because of it. He doesn't write anymore now.

Then I told a few war stories. I told the one about the asylum outside Firebase Alpha gate, and how one afternoon everyone had gone to help clean and fix the place up for the patients. And every afternoon after that the whole firebase would empty out and head over there. We'd paint and clean and hammer and nail all afternoon long. One day a general decided to come over and see his American boys performing another unselfish deed. He got over there just after we'd finished for the afternoon, just in time to see us line up for our daily reward — a shorttime with two, pretty, thirteen-year-old inmates.

Then I told how once while I was on guard duty I heard them, the VC, out there, rustling and clanking and scratching in the night. And I told how they started getting closer, until I was sure I heard them talking and laughing, like they were playing cards, and how I took the claymore mine switch and crawled down on the bunker floor because I didn't want to see them coming. I knew once they got close enough, once I heard them out in the wire, I'd be able to pull the switch. I lay there and squeezed the claymore switch for two hours. But about dawn everything stopped entirely, and I was sure that they were gone, that things were fine again, so I built up enough courage to get up and go out and pull the claymores in. But I discovered after I got out there that the mines had been turned around. I told, too, how once I got back to the company I refused to leave my tent until finally they sent me home. And then I told how I started seeing this army psychiatrist once I got back, and how the psychiatrist instructed me not to see my old friends anymore, that they had been all my trouble, that they had made me too weak to face up to the ways of the war. I told how I stopped seeing the psychiatrist instead.

New Year's Eve Mauer recited a poem he wrote once about the war. We all cheered. I seem to remember that someone even started to cry. At five to twelve we stacked some books up on the floor, and at midnight we all took turns jumping off into the new year. Mauer said he hoped there really was something new about this one, but Tom said he didn't see why this one would be any different.

We headed back the next morning, on New Year's Day. Willie had a little money he didn't need, enough for gas and coffee, and he filled the trunk and the back seat with Molson. We waved good-bye and set out at ten o'clock.

On the way back, Johnny Mathis came on the radio singing "Wonderful, Wonderful," and for a moment something flickered in all of us. I could see it on their faces in the front, in the rearview mirror, Mauer's lips drooping, Tom's eyes glassy and dreamy. We were all remembering Mauer's parents' living room as kids, listening to that song, talking about girls and the life to come. That song always seemed to be playing then, in those days, and it always inspired us to passion and awe in the face of the goodness of our young lives.

Those Johnny Mathis moments still occur once in a great while, but they pass quickly now, even more quickly than they did a year ago. A year ago, even, it may have started us talking and making new plans, promising changes. But now we all realized at once that it was too dim to remember clearly enough.

A little later Tom asked for another beer. Later still he weaved off to the shoulder of the road and the sand flew. I dozed and remembered we had been thinking ahead. We had it timed so we hit Emerson Junction again at three in the morning.

THE DIFFERENCE A TET MAKES

EVERY DAY IN the late afternoon, after their duties were completed, the men from First Company, Third Battalion, First Infantry Division at Firebase Bravo, a unit of one hundred tucked between a sharp bend in the Mekong River, went to the village of Chau-Duc, two kilometers south, on the west bank of the river. The men roared into town in their armed jeeps and atop APCs and half tracks, then spread out over the town in groups of four or five, gulping Cokes and *Ba-Muoi-Ba* at the village stands, playing with kids and street hustlers. Finally, later, they all converged on the whorehouses and blowjob parlors, five plywood and crushed beercan shacks on the edge of town. In the early evening, before dark, the men all boarded their vehicles once again and headed back to their firebase en masse. As they roared out of town, the red dust swelling about them, the whores lined up in front of the shacks, laughing and waving and jumping up and down.

* * *

The mortars and rockets began falling on Firebase Bravo at 3:02 A.M. on the twenty-third of January and continued at intervals until the thirty-first of March. Five minutes after the first mortars and rockets began, the small arms fire commenced against the two, non-naturally defended sides of the firebase. The fire continued twice a day for hour periods, every day. American 105s from nearby air bases and artillery from Firebase Bravo shelled and strafed the village of Chau-Duc twice daily until the siege was finally concluded the end of March.

* * *

After the siege was over, once the shacks had been rebuilt and the kids and the whores were back in business, the men of the First Company, Third Battalion, First Infantry Division returned to the town every late afternoon and remained there until early evening. They still bought their Cokes and *Ba-Muoi-Ba* from the village street stands; they still teased the kids and showered them with candy and gum; and they still ended up every evening out at the rebuilt whorehouses and blowjob parlors on the street entering town.

Now, however, since the siege, as they headed out of Chau-Duc amid the rumble of their vehicles, the men showed a new-found sense of humor. As they headed away in their jeeps and atop their APCs and half tracks, they swung their guns around and aimed at the girls. Some of the men made mocking pop, pop, pop shooting noises; others shook their fists good-naturedly and shouted obscenities. The girls, lined up, jumping and laughing like always, shook their tiny fists, too, and answered in kind in Vietnamese. An untouched observer perhaps, or even one of the very small children who hung close to the whorehouses and blowjob parlors, playing absentmindedly in the dirt, would have heard their good natured voices like music, the men and the whores, Vietnamese and American voices, singing through the dusk and the stars beginning to spread the sky, even above the roar of the vehicles of war, singing, blindly singing, *Du Me May* and Motherfucker cutting through the early evening Asian air like a welding of the world.

FALLING IN LOVE
AT THE END OF THE WORLD

RAY SPENT THE first three months of the war washing jeeps, trucks, and APCs in the company motorpool. As he worked, scrubbing away the mud and grime of battle, he nicknamed all his fellow American soldiers movie stars, a habit he had acquired growing up in Michigan's Upper Peninsula. Since his front teeth were so huge that he decided early in life it could only have been a celestial joke visited upon him by a sadistic, vengeful God, and since he didn't even ice skate, much less zip around the frozen, ice sculpture–rimmed lakes with a hockey stick clutched in his hand like the rest of his classmates, nor like his father trudge off every morning to the red copper mines, a black lunch pail beating his leg like the pump, pump, pump rhythm of his life, Ray spent the leaden-sky winter afternoons in the town's one movie theatre on Main Street. Movies in the U.P. were cheap then, so after school he sat warm and dry and alone as a hundred inches of snow piled up outside, watching John Wayne save the world for democracy, and naming his classmates and everyone else in town by the characters he saw move, merge, appear, and reappear across the screen like dreams. Kirk Douglas, Burt Lancaster, Alan Ladd, Richard Widmark, Robert Mitchum, William Holden, Audrey Hepburn, Ingrid Bergman, Bette Davis, Joan Crawford, Grace Kelly. He even named his parents, though, since they were reclusive and sullen, they paid little attention to their only child. Miners and miners' wives in the U.P. were mostly reclusive and sullen, except on Friday nights late when they charged drunk out of the town's three Main Street bars, in the summer to roar motorboats across the lakes like maniacs, or in the winter to tip ice fishing shacks and swill whiskey straight from the bottle like Dukhobors until dawn. But his silent parents didn't even participate in this debauchery. It was as if they had been dealt a blow from which they never recovered. Like Bogart and Bacall.

In Vietnam Ray washed vehicles and amused himself with his naming game for three months. Every day he rubbed away, all morning, all afternoon, and into the early evening. The only war he knew was walking company guard every ten days, simply strolling between the lines of tin and screen hootches from midnight until 6:00 A.M. under the perfect black sky, an M-16 over his shoulder and a helmet on his head, making certain a drunken Bill Holden didn't shoot someone on his way to the toilet from the company club. Ray washed and he named and he guarded. He kept to himself and the time flew.

Then one day, after three months, he fell in love with Hong, a company mess hall worker ten years his senior with five children, whose husband had been killed two years before near Hue, shot down in a C-123 flying too near an enemy-infested rice paddy. Ray arrived at the mess hall late one night for the evening meal, and still hadn't finished when the Vietnamese workers headed out of the kitchen, their trays piled with food. He felt violated, attacked, as he saw them come, as he watched them flood out of the backroom and surround him. Hong plopped herself down at his table without asking and began to eat.

Then, for no reason, she looked up at him and scowled as if she were about to throw up, as if merely looking at him made her want to vomit. She lashed out at him—a man—a symbol of all men, it seemed, her mouth full, rice on her lips. She berated him in pidgin English, Vietnamese, and perhaps a little Laotian and Montagnard mixed in. Her English was not particularly good, but he was amazed that he understood her perfectly anyway. He decided then and there that anyone could communicate with anyone else, if he had something horrible and abusive enough to say.

She told him men were all alike, American, Vietnamese, all men. They took everything from you and then they left you alone. They always left you alone. Her husband had left her, killed by the war, and Ray would leave his girlfriend, too, in one way or another. Like all men. Men always left, she said.

As Hong harangued him, he saw that she was not like the other Vietnamese around the company, those whom he mostly ignored as they filled sandbags and built bunkers and smoked opium on their breaks, squatting together in circles all over the compound, wizened and slope-eyed old men and women, passing long metal tube pipes from one to the other. Sometimes they stopped him in the company street and asked him to buy them American cigarettes at cut-rate PX prices, ubiquitous in their white cotton shirts and silky black pants, their smooth black hair, the men and the women exactly alike. But even though Hong had long black hair, too, her hair was not smooth and sleek like the others, but thick and loose and fluffy. Her face and hips were broader, too, and her lips thicker; he wondered as he listened to her if she were part Cambodian. He had overheard once that Cambodians were broader and thicker than the Vietnamese. He had heard it somewhere in the company, God knew where, as now he was beginning to forget all life before that very moment, all memory sucked away and out of his experience like a movie running backwards at top speed. As she picked up her rice bowl and placed it to her thick lips, shoveling in rice with her chopsticks, he fell hopelessly and inexorably in love with her.

She was loud and obnoxious with him at first. She browbeat him mercilessly and humiliated him anywhere, anytime, in front of anyone—she would tell anyone who would listen how repugnant and contemptible he was—from the time she arrived in the morning and he saw her at breakfast, until before she boarded the back of the deuce-and-a-half for the ride back to Bien-Hoa, as the other mess hall employees looked on, amused by the show appearing before them. She taught him to eat like he was supposed to eat, like the rest of them ate, and harassed him when he slipped at something. She brooked no mistakes from him, and when he fumbled with his chopsticks and lost them in his fingers or faltered at some other detail, she told him he was stupid or crazy—*dien cai dau* meant both stupid and crazy, he decided, as she yelled at him over and over again across the mess hall table. She showed him how to mix his vegetables with his rice, how to hold his bowl and put it to his mouth, how to push the food forward, and how much *nuoc-mam* to put on whatever he ate. She brought him sandwiches and *Ba-Muoi-Ba* from the market for his breakfast each morning, and she taught him to keep butter off his rice at all costs. Butter on rice? she sneered, making a horrible, distorted face. She called him *dien cai dau* and pussy face and beat on his arms.

She tested him with money. One payday she told him she needed $300.00 in American money right away and that he had to get it for her. She didn't bother to tell him why; she needed it, that was all, and he had to get it. Then, later, after he had complied with her wishes and sat suffering, wondering the rest of the long afternoon as he scrubbed vehicle after vehicle, tank and APC after tank and APC, what he would do for a whole month without a cent of spending money, even for cigarettes, she came into his hootch after work and gave him his money back. She tossed it on his bed and said she never wanted a single thing from him, ever. She swept his money onto the floor and kicked it against the wall. Who did he think he was, anyway? She stamped her foot. He mattered nothing to her, nothing at all.

She paraded before him from the mess hall to the toilet down at the end of the company street, and refused to acknowledge his presence as he stood in his hootch doorway and mooned after her, longing for her glance as she passed. As she strolled along, she swung her hips provocatively before the other Americans who stood about in doorways or lounged atop sandbag bunkers between the buildings. The others called out to her to come to them, calling her gook and whore, and cunt and bitch and slope, and she laughed and flirted more, like they sang gentle music that nurtured her soul.

Sometimes, before the deuce-and-a-half picked them up at night to take them back to their homes down the road in Bien-Hoa, she came into his hootch when she knew he was alone, sat with him on his bed and told him how much she had loved her husband and about all the other American lovers she had had. She told him what wonderful lovers they had all been. She swooned when she said it. Her eyes glazed over and rolled back into her head. He could never be as good as them, she said. He might as well forget that. She watched him suffer as she talked, until finally, she slapped her thigh and laughed in his face, then quickly headed outside to join the others in the back of the covered truck for the trip home. Sometimes, before she left, she told him she hated him beyond words, beyond belief, and sometimes she told him he mattered too little for her to even hate him. She hardly knew he existed, she said.

As the weeks and months passed, when he wasn't working, Ray spent every possible moment with the Vietnamese. He ate with them, he squatted with them behind the tin yellow mess hall during their breaks. He bought them cigarettes when they wanted and did their bidding in any other way he could. He tried to make himself useful as Hong pointed and rattled off amusing anecdotes and fantasies about him to the others, stupid things he had said or done, and things she made up. He grinned sheepishly as the others laughed at him and beat their thighs. He tried to understand their language as they talked, to pick up a word here or there by gesture and association. They laughed at him often and told him if he continued to eat so much *nuoc-mam* and drink *Ba-Muoi-Ba*, his skin would yellow and his eyes would slope. He gorged himself even more, day and night, and looked for telltale signs every morning in his wall locker mirror. He would have taken a bath in *nuoc-mam* if he could have arranged it.

Eventually he got permission to ride in the back of the deuce-and-a-half to Bien Hoa every evening as their gunner, their lone protection from the shadows in the night, as the truck roared at top speed down the road toward town. As time passed, for their amusement, he brandished his weapon like an Apache from a cowboy and Indian movie and even fired off a few rounds across the dark open rice paddies, the red tracer rounds veering off and dying in the darkness out beyond the lights of the truck, the darkness at the end of the world. Their exotic eyes, their open laughing mouths, and strange Asian smells intoxicated him. Every night, once the truck halted at the gate, he wished with all his heart to descend and disappear forever into Bien-Hoa with Hong and the others.

* * *

Then one day, without warning, Hong changed. She began to treat him gently and with tenderness. She came around to his hootch every night before the truck pulled out for Bien-Hoa—she even stayed so long now that they often had to run to catch it. She sat on his bed and asked about his life in America, his family, his mother and his father. Where was Michigan and what was it like there? Was it near Chicago? She had heard of Chicago, of course. He was an only child. Where were his brothers and sisters? Was something wrong with his parents?

Ray had no idea why she suddenly stopped flirting with other Americans, but he accepted this amazing change, too, like he was learning to accept everything, like he accepted B-52s off the perimeter tipping and shaking the world, and artillery booming long into the night, like he accepted the hot sun in the dry season, and the torrential rains in the monsoon. Now, as Hong passed toward the toilet, she kept her eyes trained on Ray and ignored the others when they called out to her. She laughed when he said something funny and listened when he talked. She stopped ridiculing him before the other Vietnamese as they squatted behind the mess hall or as they ate their meals after the other Americans had left. And she stopped taking his money, even for a second just to tease him.

As they sat together side by side in his hootch one day, she even talked about her own life, her parents, her dead husband, and her five children. They had lived in Hue before her husband had been killed; they were from near Hue, a tiny village called Tran-May. They had grown up together and married and had a good life. Until he was killed.

As she talked, Ray could see green flooded paddies stretched flat for miles, water buffalo moving slowly across the horizon, men beating them gently with sticks, buses to Hue with Hong and her mother on Saturday afternoons, the buses crowded with Vietnamese women heading to the market and then home again, laden with bamboo tote bags of fruit and vegetables and live chickens tied upside down by their feet, the bus popping and bouncing down the broken road, belching oil, driving the chickens into flopping, squawking frenzy. He watched Hong's beautiful face and listened to her talk of her past without regret.

Her husband had been lucky enough to go to flight school when he went into the air force and became a pilot. His father had been a special friend of the village chief, and the village chief knew someone in Saigon. Her husband had been lucky, she said.

Hong stopped and placed her hand over Ray's. She turned away and looked at the wall. She shook her head. But one day her husband went out and didn't come back.

Ray listened and watched the last of the sun shine like a high school bonfire off the tin hootch across from his own. Three 105s fired up, blasting down the runway. Hong turned to him, and once the noise died, she continued. Ray listened to her spread her life out before him like a strategist spreading a map before the eyes of his troops, and he wept.

Then she invited him to meet her in town that next Thursday. Every Thursday was her day off, as he well knew — the longest days of his life, interminable days, the dirty vehicles multiplied endlessly in the bright merciless Asian sun as the days wore on into night. And if he could arrange it somehow, she said, she would meet him in the park behind the Bien-Hoa Provincial Hospital. He couldn't miss it: The hospital had a bell tower, and was the largest building in town. He'd arrange it, he said.

The hospital was a whitewashed, stucco building on a tree-lined boulevard next to the Bien-Hoa Tennis Club. As Ray approached, he could hear balls bouncing back and forth across the nets from player to player. The players were all old and skinny and rich in their baggy white shorts, and Ray watched them play flawlessly from behind the screen gate. No ball ever dribbled over the net or pinged off the fence unreturned. They volleyed on and on until he turned and walked to the hospital and stood under the archway entrance. Up close he could see that the hospital had turned pink from endless sand and dust assaults. He looked up at the dusty bell suspended above and knew telepathically why the bell was there, why a bell was suspended above a hospital archway: The hospital had been a Catholic church during the French occupation. It was a good omen, he decided.

In the park was an orange and white pagoda and five other smaller monuments nestled in the tall grass like they had all fallen from the sky. When he saw Hong—he had come around a tree and come upon her sitting on a black bench near a food stand —she surprised him. She wore a snow white *ao-dai* and Ray stopped before she saw him and held his breath, afraid she too had fallen from the sky.

It turned out that the person who ran the food stand was a pockmarked woman with black stained teeth named Phuong, and that she was a friend of Hong's. They had known each other since Hong had come to town from Hue two years before. Phoung's husband was also dead, and their children were friends, too, and roamed the Bien-Hoa streets together. Hong and Phuong commiserated with each other often about their children and what was becoming of them.

That first afternoon, as soon as Ray sat on the bench next to Hong, she hit him on the arm and told him she hated him again. He had a new lover, she told him, in Bien-Hoa. Phuong had told her so just that morning. Phuong had seen him in a bar with his arm around a new girl, whispering and laughing, even kissing. The New York Bar; that was the one.

Phuong looked at Ray, shrugged her shoulders, and shook her head. Don't worry, Hong was crazy, she said. Hong was *dien cai dau*.

Ray had been warned by the other mess hall workers that morning what would await him. Hong would tease him horribly, they said, but he shouldn't worry. It was just part of the courting ritual. Ray should play along. It was best to do this, it was best to do that, they told him. They trained him; they rehearsed that morning during breakfast for the real thing that afternoon. One of the women took Hong's place. They urged him; they pushed him forward, helping him with his lines, the men prompting him and having the time of their lives at his expense. Finally he was ready. He'd be fine, they said.

So Ray responded as they had taught him. Yes, he had a new girlfriend, three in fact—one in the New York Bar and two more across the street, in the Nha-Trang Bar. But he liked the one in the New York best of all. He was particularly fond of her. Yes, it was true. He was in love and soon he would ask her to marry him.

Hong shook her hair to one side and laughed in a way Ray had not heard her laugh before, like young women laughed with lovers on the streets of the Upper Peninsula when he was a small boy. He was clever all right, Hong said. He knew everything. She pounded her thigh and laughed again. She pushed him away from her and talked rapidly to Phuong.

As the weeks passed Ray came to see Hong every Thursday afternoon. At first the three of them continued with a combination of pidgin English and a few Vietnamese words, but eventually they taught him even more Vietnamese words. They taught him the word for rice seedling and for sandwich and for love. They taught him the words for child and husband and lover and for good, for bad, and for war. Until he learned their complicated language, and he learned it rapidly, like he had been touched. They gave him books and a dictionary to study in bed the long nights away from Hong. Phuong smiled at him through beetlenut-stained teeth as he spoke and learned, and Hong became more beautiful as the days passed. Like magic, the more words he learned, the more beautiful she became.

It was at this time, too, that Ray began to read books from the company library—a tiny collection in the corner of the orderly room on a three row bookshelf, donated for the edification of the soldiers by various groups in America. He read these books along with his Vietnamese ones; it passed the long nights without Hong more quickly than before. Reading was something he had done little of growing up in Michigan; he had been too much in movie houses. But these books told him many things. *Fire in the Lake*, for example, told him not to be deceived, that learning Vietnamese brought him no closer to the people he loved; he would always be a dupe, an outsider. *Street without Joy* told him that he should be on his guard because things were never what they seemed to him; he was a fool to be so happy in this place. He must look—it was his duty. He must find unhappiness where he could find it.

But soon Ray and Hong were meeting at night, too, every night. He stopped riding with them to town in the deuce-and-a-half, but instead walked the long way, three miles across the air base to the back gate. He moved as quickly as he could over the flat dusty base roads, down past the dispensary hootch, past the gate to the 135th LURP Camp, alone and mysterious out on the edge of the perimeter, past the air base runways and parking shelters filled with 105s and Cobra gunships, always on the verge of rising up alive and heading out into the war. He met Hong on the main street of town, and they walked together to meet Phuong in the park.

And then one night, just before Ray rose to leave and return to the air base for another lonely night, Hong touched his hand and whispered. She kissed his cheek for the first time like wet feathers and whispered, *Em yeu em*, I love you, so softly he wasn't sure he heard and had to have her repeat it at least ten times.

On his way back to the company that night firecrackers were thrown into the air and rolled at his feet. People moved throughout the city, drinking and dancing and crying in the night. As he continued on toward the gate, the world was filled with music, and he felt himself shaken to his boots with Asia. But just then, just as he entered the company, the siren he had never heard before but would hear oh so many times again began to wail, and he ran and ran and ran while the mortars and rockets fell and fell and fell.

* * *

And he remembered he knew for certain he would die after that first attack siren but he did not die, and he couldn't count the number of times after that that he wished death on all Vietnamese everywhere, once Tet exploded in the night and they were under siege, and there were no longer any Vietnamese anywhere but those out there beyond that perimeter who wanted to kill and torture and mutilate him in ways he couldn't even bear to consider, so he stopped seeing Americans as movie stars once the first rocket fell, once the first rattle of small arms fire began—he knew he had merely been arrogant and self-righteous and his brief love affair with Hong had been nothing but youthful illusion, even though he could not stop dreaming of her, of seeing her standing still among the rubble of the park, among the twisted, charred remains of Phuong's food stand, until she saw him and disappeared down an alley, walked rapidly out of his life forever and left him knee deep among the ruins where he had been in love for the first time—and so he became friends with every American he met, and finally became one of the guys, and they all got drunk together deep in their bunkers every night, dreaming how wonderful it would be when they got back to the world where there were no bunkers, no smell of *nuoc-mam*, insecticide, gunpowder and burning shit, and he began to wait and hope and beg for his own Freedom Bird, until he actually imagined how it would be as the years passed when he would forget everything that ever happened to him, until Vietnam seemed somehow not of this world or had maybe been told to him long ago by someone he once knew but no longer cared about and never wished to see again.

DOGS

ONE DAY THE dogs came. There were four of them, and they walked purposefully into the company en masse, unannounced, and sat down in front of the mess tent as if they had been summoned for a terribly important mission.

There was Shorttime, snow white, arrogant, and promiscuous, who gravitated immediately to the officers' hootch; Blackdog, the shaggy, low-to-the-ground fighter who stalked the company and liked the motorpool workers best; Ky, sandy and sheepish, wily and refined—the interpreters took him; and idiosyncratic, loud-mouthed Shaky—minus a back leg—the NCOs' favorite.

Each group patted and caressed and fawned over their dogs. Soon, they occupied all the men's waking hours. And the dogs followed their masters closely, sniffing at their heels, waiting for orders.

Eventually jealousies and fist fights broke out. And the dogs began fighting, too. Even Shaky hobbled into the fray. They snapped and growled and snarled.

One day they left as they had come. They all walked off together, single file, as if they had finished their important work and were needed no longer. They moved down the dusty base road, off the end of the base like off the end of the world, and disappeared.

The American soldiers watched them go and were sad for weeks. The Vietnamese workers never even noticed they were gone.

LAN'S WORLD

I WORKED MIDNIGHT to ten my first five months in Vietnam, translating messages that sounded more like letters home, even love letters, than enemy plots and activities.

"23 November. Dear Xuan, Situation normal. No enemy activity. How is Thuy? Tell her I miss her. And tell Bac I miss her, too, Love, Lang."

After work, rather than go to bed, I remember walking the two miles across the dusty air base, past rows of metal hootches, gray-tin sandbagged bunkers, Mamasans—conical hats wobbling—Huey gunships and F-105s with teeth on the tips, dripping painted blood, out past the MP gate, into Bien-Hoa. I remember sitting in bars until late afternoon, the wild red and purple honky tonk, incense and sweet Asian perfume, hot, sexy and exotic other-worldly, drinking *Ba-Muoi-Ba*, harassing girls in mini-skirts, tiny sashaying behinds, ignoring their repeated demands for Saigon Teas, sharpening my language skills on their shrill, screeching voices. I called myself Nhu, a name given to me by Ong Son, one of my teachers in language school. All the girls picked up on the name quickly, and I became known in that small, ravished, once-upon-a-time city as one of those unusual Americans who spoke their language.

In the late afternoon, before heading back to the company to bed, if I were not too weary—and I was hardly ever too weary—I walked down a well-known, well-worn alley to a blowjob parlor or whorehouse, among the jaded, lounging, chattering girls, into twisted, dirty, smelly, sweaty sheets. The first week I reveled in the filth with a particularly small, pock-faced sixteen-year-old, limbs like a partridge, originally from Hue, who for another 500 piasters, tolerated my questions about Central Vietnamese slang. And I remember that once I began frequenting that alley, lost my "whoring virginity," so to speak, I was glad it was over, happy it was gone.

And then one morning, after three months, I stopped going to the bars or the whorehouses or the blowjob parlors. For reasons I still don't understand—I really don't think there were reasons for most of the things I did—that morning I suddenly walked off the main street and headed toward the Bien-Hoa Provincial Hospital bell tower. There was a park directly across the street from the hospital and I was shocked that there was a park there, in Bien-Hoa, in Vietnam, in the midst of all the whoring and drinking and war making. I remember walking by the benches and fruit stands and the large, broken-down orange and white pagoda for the first time and wondering if a spell had passed over me.

I sat down on a bench facing the hospital so I could be in the shade of the park and look up at the white, French-built hospital, decaying in the fierce late morning sun, the walls gouged and broken, no bell any longer in the bell tower. A cement fence surrounding the hospital ended at a metal gate in front, creating a courtyard around the two main buildings. Vietnamese milled about the gate, entering and exiting at will, the ARVN MP guard ignoring the world in front of him, his carbine slung over his shoulder, the small barrel extending above his back like a metal extension out of his body. I remember gray, blood-soaked bandages, heads, arms, legs, crutches, sticks for canes, legless human beings sliding along the ground like huge, unfamiliar animals.

I felt my bench move and turned to see an eleven-year-old Vietnamese girl, in a dirt- and dust-streaked white blouse, a conical hat and filthy black pants. I nearly wept as her small face burst into Kathleen's smile.

When I think of Lan now, I think of her in relation to myself, my consummate naïveté. And she acted like an innocent for me, like a little girl playing hooky, rather than one absolutely alone in the world, struggling daily to exist.

Day after day, I would ask her why she wasn't in school, would exhort her to go to school. And she would say, oh yes, and smile Kathleen's smile. She would go tomorrow, tomorrow for sure. And she was always so cheerful, lying to me as I wished to be lied to, until I gave her what she waited patiently for, her daily 500 piasters. Yes, she knew she should go to school and she would sometime soon. And Kathleen's smile would make me feel real, focused for another day.

I know now, of course, that she was just one of those thousands of kids with no parents, fending for themselves on the streets of Vietnam. She had somehow, even in that corrupt, riddled, forever war-torn land, endeared herself to the doctors and nurses at the hospital—perhaps the magic of Kathleen's smile had worked on them too—and they allowed her to sleep inside the gate until six A.M. During those two months of morning meetings, I never knew her to stray more than a block from the hospital, always clinging, it appeared, closely to the center of her small universe. Or so I thought then as I watched her and talked to her day in and day out. The incongruity of Kathleen's smile in the face of an eleven-year-old Vietnamese girl amazes me no more now than it did then.

Our relationship continued unbroken for those two months, until one night—again without reason—it suddenly came into my head, after leaving the mess hall, to return to town to blowjob alley and stop at a place where I'd never been before, one with an unusually seedy reputation—even there—a particularly hard and often violent place frequented by those in from long, horror-filled weeks in the field. All I can imagine is that I must have been feeling a great need for degradation and fear.

I remember that it was late, seven forty-five, uncomfortably close to eleven o'clock curfew with the long walk back. The night was a busy one and I had to wait for one of the girls to finish before taking my turn. And suddenly Lan walked out of the back room with a Special Forces captain behind her. I remember him better than I remember this morning's breakfast, a giant, hulking man, a yellowing, fading scar beneath his left eye all the way down below the neckline of his fatigue shirt. He grinned at me, a wide, nicotine-stained grin from the mouth of death, and his scar actually jumped. He placed a huge hand on Lan's tiny head, covering it all the way down to her little nose. "Best little babysan blowjob in Nam." Lan looked at me and smiled hard and proud and condescending, narrowing her black eyes. "This is the way things are," she seemed to say to me. "And nothing you can do can change them."

A week later Tet began and town was closed to us forever.

Rick Christman was born, raised, and educated in the public schools in north central Wisconsin. He received a B.A. in philosophy from the University of Wisconsin-Madison, an M.A. in English from Mankato State University, and a D.A. in English from Drake University. His stories have been published in literary magazines throughout the country, including *Indiana Review, Wormwood Review, Great River Review, River City Review, Z Miscellaneous,* and *Touchstone.* He has also won a number of grants and awards, including a University of Wisconsin-Madison George B. Hill Memorial Award and a Loft-McKnight Award in Fiction. He teaches writing and literature at the Ankeny campus of Des Moines Area Community College, and lives in Des Moines, Iowa.

About his writing, Christman says: "Writing is the opportunity to create worlds, worlds that have not existed until the writer creates them. I believe that my stories are worlds according to Rick Christman, and I trust my readers to want to enter those worlds, to make them part of their own reality."